T0339461

# Head, Heart, and Hands Listening in Coach Practice

This book is an exploration of intentional listening as an essential skill for coaches. It introduces the Head, Heart, and Hands Listening model as a vital tool to amplify effective listening in coaching practice.

Accessible and applicable, the book explores the three listening modalities of Head, Heart, and Hands as active, though largely unconscious, lenses that inform the potency of our listening. Dakin-Neal argues that once coaches identify "how" they listen, they can assist their clients in more targeted ways to positively impact their personal and professional lives. Chapters are divided into the three listening modalities, Head, Heart, and Hands, and are filled with case studies, stories, reflective questions, and exercises from the author's experience to help coaches strengthen their listening skills. The book also includes a comprehensive listening assessment for coaches to use in practice.

This book is essential reading for coaches in practice and in training as well as organizational psychologists, HR professionals, and those working within corporations.

**Kymberly Dakin-Neal, MEd**, is a mindset coach, playback practitioner, and founder of Voice into Learning, LLC. Her specialty is team experience design with individual coaching programs and applied mediums like improvisation, intentional listening, and focused creativity.

"Listening is what the world needs more of. Deep listening transforms and enriches all our relationships and work. It is also at the core of effective coaching. Coaches and clients alike can learn to deepen their listening and overall communication skills with Dakin-Neal's holistic Head, Heart, and Hands approach. I appreciate how the author weaves both her professional and personal experiences and insights into the book. It has an accessible feel and it's easy to 'listen' to the author. This book offers great support and guidance for being the best listener you can be!"

**Lynda Monk**, *Writing for Wellness coach; author and director of the International Association for Journal Writing*

"I've been coaching for over twenty years and was blown away by this much needed book. As coaches and therapists, we study and practice listening, but never have I encountered a resource that focuses solely and so effectively on how to do so with fresh ears and a truly unbiased perspective. This book is a must-read whether you are just starting out in the field and want to avoid the pitfalls so many of us encounter, or you've been at it for thirty years and need to heighten and deepen your awareness to ensure you haven't inadvertently started 'phoning it in.'"

**Rahti Gorfien, PCC, ACCG, CSS**, *Creative Calling Coaching, LLC*

# Head, Heart, and Hands Listening in Coach Practice

## The Listening Coach

Kymberly Dakin-Neal

Routledge
Taylor & Francis Group

NEW YORK AND LONDON

Designed cover image: © Getty Images

First published 2024
by Routledge
605 Third Avenue, New York, NY 10158

and by Routledge
4 Park Square, Milton Park, Abingdon, Oxon, OX14 4RN

*Routledge is an imprint of the Taylor & Francis Group, an informa business*

ISBN: 978-1-032-28272-5 (hbk)
ISBN: 978-1-032-28271-8 (pbk)
ISBN: 978-1-003-29602-7 (ebk)

DOI: 10.4324/9781003296027

Typeset in Optima
by Apex CoVantage, LLC

# Contents

# The Listening Coach

## Using Head, Heart, and Hands Listening in Coach Practice

### *Introduction: Why a Book About Listening?*

Blake turns off the pavement onto a dirt road leading toward dense woods. He takes a deep breath to calm his nerves and scans the landscape in front of him: scrub brush gives way to lush pine forest, and the distant blue mountains beyond disappear the deeper into the woods he goes. The road ends at the next turn. He stops the Jeep in a driveway choked with crabgrass, weeds, cigarette butts. And there he is – MJ Robbins: broad shouldered, glowering, arms crossed, stance wide. MJ is not happy. Blake wants to throw the Jeep into reverse and get the hell out, but he doesn't. It's his job to talk to MJ. It's his job to get MJ onboard with the new environmental rules on wetlands preservation. Blake needs to establish some kind of trust in the next hour that will change MJ's mind about Blake, government regulation, and environmental responsibility. But how?

Blake was, at the time of the training, in his early 30s and relatively new to the field. In our beginning sessions, he sat slouched in the back of the room, looking miserable. But when I asked for someone to volunteer a situation that we could process, his was the first hand raised. As he relayed his experience with MJ, I could see heads nodding around the room as the other trainees listened – they had all been in similar situations. I could hear the frustration in Blake's voice and a fair amount of resentment. I offered Blake a chance for a "do-over" role play with my colleague Robert so that we could analyze the situation and come up with more effective strategies. It quickly became clear what Blake was listening for: a chance to share his extensive knowledge of environmental codes and policies. But that was not the information that would get him to his ultimate goal.

Eventually, over time, Blake learned to listen for and tease out very different kinds of information: opportunities to build alliance and trust, strategies to slow himself down long enough to get curious about a landowner's deeper motivations. This made him much more effective in his work and, by extension, amplified Blake's own job satisfaction as well.

We know we need to be "good listeners", but what does that really mean? And why, in Blake's situation, was a very specific kind of listening the tool that made all the difference for Blake in connecting with landowners like MJ?

It's my intention to give you some answers to this question and a few more. The fact that you're curious enough about the topic to pick up this book tells me that you are a few steps ahead of many on the quest to dig deeper into effective listening.

In our loud and frenzied western culture, listening appears to be an assumed skill. As long as there's nothing wrong with our ears, we believe we can listen. For decades we've been fascinated by learning styles, communication styles, even styles in intelligence. I've come to believe that *how* we listen and, more importantly, what we listen *for* is foundational to whatever "style" we may possess.

Many of us in the adult learning space, and in multiple corporate programs, have also had training in "active listening": a total focus on what the speaker is saying, using all five senses, communicating nonverbally to the speaker that we are paying attention. While I find nothing wrong with this effort, I believe many of us have distilled active listening into "acting like we're listening" . . . at least until we can jump in and get others to listen to us.

Perhaps you too have become aware that we're not living in times that encourage us to listen to each other more proactively. We're continually offered opportunities via social media to bray at each other about . . . pick anything. Politics! Culture Wars! The latest tirade on Twitter! This book offers an invitation to slow down, to take a breath, to begin to notice what we pick up from the people we engage with regardless of and, in some cases, because of the way we feel about them.

I am a trainer and facilitator with a master's degree and 20 years in the field of adult learning. For much of that time, my specialty has been team experience design. The intricacies of adult listening have intrigued me for years, and I've developed the material I'm about to share with you over the course of a decade. The stories here are pulled from my experience as a coach, trainer, facilitator, and theatre improviser. All names are changed, of course, to protect privacy. It's my hope that what you read in these pages will inspire deeper curiosity, as I believe curiosity is where good listening truly begins.

I am often hired as a communications coach. A few years ago I got a chance to work with my state's Department of Environmental Protection (DEP). Their field technicians, Blake among them, were having difficulty in conversations with landowners in violation of environmental codes having to do with a wide range of issues: water pollution, wetlands preservation, pesticides, and so on. Blake's story was fairly typical of the tone in these "discussions". Some of them included large dogs. Some of them included firearms. In listening to the fears and frustrations that Blake and his colleagues shared, I got the feeling early on that communication wasn't really the foundational issue. It wasn't a matter of getting the landowners to listen. I needed to train the field techs to listen better.

I got curious. The same way any profession has occupational hazards, could there also be particular ways of listening that become more pronounced the longer we stay in a given field? Were there natural tendencies in all of us to listen for specific kinds of information, maybe the kind we know what to do with, while missing other messages that called on skills not as familiar to us? In the same way we have learning and communication styles, could we also have listening styles?

As adults, the way we listen and what we listen for could well be influenced by our profession.

I recently discovered a new term: "deformation professionale". It's a French phrase that has to do with how one's occupation skews a person's worldview – to such a degree that "information" becomes "deformation", or rather anti-information. When it comes to listening, if we are in the clutches of deformation professionale, we filter out whatever does not resonate with the worldview informed by our profession. It's not even a conscious process – it's an unconscious habit. It makes me wonder, once this term takes hold, if we will be tossing around terms like "deformation professionale syndrome". Avoiding the consequences of this habitual filter is one reason I undertook the writing of this book and endeavored to outline specifically the advantages and disadvantages of Head, Heart, and Hands listening.

Social workers, medical practitioners, and psychiatrists might employ the empathic Heart listening, whereas city planners, transportation professionals, and lawyers would land heavily on the problem-solving skills that we'll call Hands listening.

The DEP field techs, as scientists and data geeks, proved very adept Head listeners. They actively listened for opportunities to share their granular knowledge and skill to convince landowners to change their ways.

So here's a question – if a land owner is bound and determined to pave over that swampy stinky wetland in the backyard in order to expand his auto repair business, how well are facts going to work in convincing him otherwise? As Blake discovered . . . not so much.

We're awash in facts. As a culture, facts are something we increasingly tune out, and too much information often makes us feel overwhelmed. If we want to get someone to take a particular action – say, convince a loved one to change their unhealthy eating habits or a customer to purchase pricier fire-retardant materials because they will prove to be a much better value over time . . . or a patient to get the Covid vaccine, we need to begin listening for something else in these situations.

What's that "something else"? Within the pages of this book, you'll discover some answers.

You'll find new ways to apply listening as an intentional skill – one we use daily that can enrich our experience and amplify our value in any given situation. We'll dive into the three modalities in listening: Head, Heart, and Hands, foundational to the Waldorf education model, that I'll apply in this book for coaching and adult learning sensibilities. You'll encounter new information, stories, and experiments to try here, but you won't find a linear training regimen or a proven curriculum. I've written this book to inspire you to explore your intentions around listening – and how we all utilize this skill relative to how we process information. If you come to better appreciate the specific listening modalities you already use while gaining some skill and a better appreciation for those modes you struggle to access, I'll consider my job done.

Here's a quick template to guide you into the model we'll be using. Think of this as an eagle's-eye view of what we will uncover: the clouds below you clear, and beneath your wings you suddenly see a new complex structure below. It may not make sense to you right away, but the closer in you get, the clearer the architecture becomes.

# Head, Heart, and Hands Model Overview

*Head Listeners Listen for:*

- Rational function: Facts, numbers, anything that can be measured
- The known: Established patterns, what's been proven to be true
- Timeframe: The past

*Head Listeners Are Curious About . . .*
- How something works
- Linear progressions
- The factual truth: "What, where, when, and how"

*Heart Listeners Listen for:*

- Emotional context
- Opportunities to build relationship and express empathy
- The truth beneath the words
- Vocalics, body language, facial expressions
- Timeframe: The present – what is happening right now

*Heart Listeners Are Curious About . . .*
- How someone really feels
- The emotional context that informs a situation

*Hands Listeners Listen for . . .*
- Problems to solve
- Actions to take
- A strategy
- New possibilities
- The future

*Hands Listeners Are Curious About . . .*
- What hasn't been tried yet?
- What else might work?
- Work-arounds
- The "how" in solving a problem

My intention is to reference and reinforce these elements so that you, as a coach, can clarify your own listening within your practice while also giving you tools to spark curiosity in clients around their own listening. It is my belief, reinforced by experience, that the more we tune in to the information we miss as we listen and intentionally build skill in tuning in to that information, the more balanced and productive we can become in our personal and professional interactions.

On the subject of interactions, it is my hope that tools in this book will help calm the emotional reactivity in so many of our clients' problematic conversations. The tone and tenor of our cultural discourse has become increasingly toxic and stressful; this has amplified the stress and pain for many of our clients. I will share specific tools and relevant questions that align with the listening modalities in the chapters so that you, the coach, can help your clients lower the temperature on their important interactions and improve the nature of their relationships.

Additionally, you may find yourself curious about the Waldorf model of early childhood education,[1] as well as the concept and practice of Whole Body listening.[2] I won't be going into detail about these in this book, but there are copious resources available to you online.

Also, because I've found a great deal of alignment with the program that trained me as a coach, I will offer insights from the Positive Intelligence model at relevant junctures. It is my hope that you will discover similar alignment with your own model of practice. https://www. positiveintelligence.com/program/

This book will also include what I consider an essential addition to any text on listening for coach practice in particular – the art of asking interesting questions. This is, of course, already the exclusive focus of a number of very fine books. Intentional, productive listening requires the ability to ask questions that will help you quickly build trust and get off the surface with your clients in a way that makes best use of their allotted time with you. At the end of each of the Head, Heart, and Hands modality sections, I'll include a list of "Probing Questions" I have found useful in engaging a particular modality. Many of these questions will overlap, but depending on the modality, the answers will be very different.

Finally, I'll reinforce what I've already mentioned about the stories in this book: They are based on real-life cases, clients, and entities I've worked with, but any identifying details like names, locations, companies, and so on have been changed or left intentionally vague. The two exceptions to this are in the section on Make Shift Coffee House in Chapter 20 and the Restorative Justice reference in Chapter 23.

I'm glad you're here, and I'm excited for the insights you'll discover in reading *The Listening Coach: Using Head, Heart, and Hands Listening in Coach Practice*!

## Notes

1   Waldorf Model of Early Childhood Education: www.waldorfeducation.org/waldorf-education
2   Whole Body Listening: https://study.com/learn/lesson/whole-body-listening-components-examples.html

# Glossary

**Analogous Field Thinking:** The intentional sourcing of innovative ideas and solutions from a variety of outside and seemingly unrelated fields.

**Assume Positive Intent:** The belief that we're all doing the best we can.

**Binary:** The human predilection for reducing complexity into good and bad categories.

**Confirmation Bias:** The tendency to interpret new information as in alignment with our preexisting beliefs and completely tune out or discount facts that conflict with those beliefs.

**Deep Canvassing:** Canvassing that uses long empathic conversations to help shift someone's beliefs.

**Deformation Professionale:** A habitual and largely unconscious method of listening and retaining information, feeding a worldview informed by our profession.

**Empathy Map:** A visualization tool used to articulate what is known about a product user or an employee. This tool helps build a broader understanding of the "why" aspect behind needs and wants.

**Epistemic Curiosity:** A predictor of creative problem solving and creative performance.

**Expectancy Bias:** Seeing and hearing new information within the boundaries of one's established expectations.

**Fixed vs. Growth Mindsets:** Identified by Carol Dweck as our belief that abilities are innate and therefore immutable (fixed) or able to be cultivated with practice and intentionality (growth).

**Groupthink:** The practice of thinking or making decisions as a group in a way that discourages creativity or individual responsibility.

**Listening Modality:** A perception style directing what we hear towards Head, Heart, or Hands listening.

**Lizard Brain:** The part of the brain to which primitive, non-rational, self-interested behavior is attributed.

**Mirror Neurons:** Neurons that fire both when a person acts and when another person observes the same action. The neuron "mirrors" the behavior of the other, as though the observer were itself acting.

**Motivational Interview:** A collaborative, person-centered form of guiding to elicit and strengthen motivation for change.

**Multidimensional Perfectionism:** Self-oriented perfectionism (expectations of perfecting oneself), socially prescribed perfectionism (perceived perfection from social media and the surrounding culture), and other-oriented perfectionism (perfection demanded of others).

**Quiet Quitting:** Doing less at work – perhaps refusing to work overtime or answer emails outside of work hours. It is in reaction to the hustle-culture mentality that work has to be the singular focus of one's life. It promotes the view that a person's worth is not defined by their job.

**Reactance:** The active and often hostile reaction to change that is demanded from outside authorities.

**Saboteurs:** From the Positive Intelligence model: entities operating within us built on positive qualities that, when overused, become counterproductive and result in problematic behavior defaults.

**Serendipity:** The occurrence and development of events by chance in a happy or beneficial way.

**Service Exchange:** The exchange of services or bartering activity across a large community network.

**Social Capital:** A concept in social science that involves the potential of individuals to secure benefits and invent solutions to problems through membership in social networks.

**Sociometrics:** The quantitative study and measurement of relationships within a group of people. Prompted by specific questions, participants in a group are asked to respond any number of physical ways: placing themselves at different locations within a circle, for example, or facing forward or backward in a line.

**Speech-Thought Differential:** The difference in our rate of speaking versus our rate of thinking.

# PART

## 1

# Learning to Pay a New Kind of Attention

# Dave's Story

## The Limits of Traditional Leadership Listening

I spent five years working in a local non-profit service exchange. Our primary mission was to encourage members to consider their skills valuable in exchange for a variety of needed services, most of which could be provided by other members. We operated a network of locally situated service exchanges with individuals as well as establishing partnerships with community nonprofits and small businesses. The exchange grew quickly over a period of about five years, but we had just lost our very charismatic executive director to the real estate business. In addition, the founder, and primary revenue source, was increasingly adamant that we needed to become self-sustaining.

Those of us in our respective jobs – I was outreach and training coordinator – were exclusively women. After a six-month search, the principal funder decided to hire "Dave". Dave had a business background. He owned and successfully grew a portfolio of fast food franchises in the midwestern state that he came from.

Entering into our workplace culture, Dave found himself on a very different planet. For those of us already working there, it became clear, with Dave's hiring, that our mission had become one of organizational sustainability rather than the exclusive focus on addressing community needs. Many of the staff had been in their positions for almost ten years. They were dedicated to helping build community sustainability through a service exchange model, but organizational sustainability had not been a priority. No one was comfortable with the changes signaled by Dave's hiring. In fact, within a few week's time, there was outright hostility. The

DOI: 10.4324/9781003296027-2

situation ultimately taught me a great deal about the peculiar passive-aggression that can erupt in some female-dominated workplaces under the stress of needed change.

Because I genuinely liked Dave and understood what he was trying to do, I was afforded a "middle woman" position between factions. My focus became largely about helping the staff work through this impasse.

Dave did his best, but his background had not prepared him to deal with this particular toxic dynamic. Staff meetings would go something like this:

An enthusiastic Dave begins with "Hey there! Thanks for coming in this morning, and I hope we can wrap this up in no more than 45 minutes, cause we all have things to do – right?"

Silence. Someone (Cathy) coughs. Dave moves on. He turns to the vivid charts he's put together on our membership numbers, our income, and our outlay over the last quarter. All but the third category have red arrows pointing down. "Looks like we have some work to do – right?" He continues explaining the stats and making the case for increasing both our membership numbers as well as the annual membership fee in order to balance what we have spent on numerous community projects. There is really no disputing the numbers.

I look around to gauge the group reaction: Cathy looks down at the table, Rhonda looks up at the ceiling. Michelle, Liz, and Taylor are glaring at Dave. He asks "So . . . anyone have any ideas on how we can get out of the red?" Again, he's met with silence. He's working very hard to contain his frustration. The team pushes back with their concerns: in the past, the founder has taken care of any financial discrepancies; members will quit if they have to pay more; more members will ultimately mean more staff hiring; and so on. Dave counters with "We all agreed at the start of the year that this organization needs to become sustainable, as the founder can't support it indefinitely. This is the reality we have to work with."

More awkward silence. Rhonda looks at her watch. "Uhm. Dave, I have to meet with our tech guy in 10 minutes and I need to prep." Dave takes a deep breath. "Okay, I know we're at time, but can I at least ask you to come back next week with some workable possibilities?" Tired heads nod, he gets a few murmurs of "Okay", and everyone trudges out of the room.

He had tried hard to engage everyone involved in his idea of productive dialogue, but Dave was stymied by the muted response he received, along with the staff tendency to nod their heads in meetings and then do things exactly the way they always had. Little was accomplished. Dave became more and more frustrated and understandably irritable with the rest of the staff. This just made the situation worse, of course, as everything Dave said and did was now fed through the defensive filter of the women's negative expectations. They felt bullied and unheard; they clearly thought he did not understand or appreciate the organization's foundational mission. And a black-and-white, good-and-bad, all-or-nothing binary set in.

This dynamic was on track to make everyone's participation, no matter how committed, much more difficult.

Finally, one Monday morning, our staff meeting started differently. No charts, no red arrows. Dave wasn't standing, he sat down with us. He took a deep breath, and began.

> "I know these last weeks have been really difficult for you. And I haven't made it easy." I heard Rhonda take a deep breath. Dave continues. "I'm also aware that many, maybe most of you, don't feel as if your concerns have been heard by me, or by [the founder]." Michelle widens her eyes and looks down at the table. No one speaks. Dave clears his throat. "Well, that changes as of today." He takes a deep breath. "I'm asking for your help. I want you to know that I am listening. Please help me understand what I am missing."

It took awhile, and a bit more prompting from Dave, but eventually, each staff member shared a litany of concerns, member stories of both hardship and success, vital programs that needed to be fully funded, not cut in the interests of sustainability. Dave would ask a clarifying question, but he mostly stayed quiet, wrote down some notes, and thanked each person for their input, even if it was uncomfortable to hear. The meeting took three hours. Everyone was pleased when he treated us all to lunch.

It's interesting what happens when the target of our animosity is suddenly vulnerable and authentic. We are faced with a choice: we can engage in healing the relationship to improve the situation, or we can instead continue to invest in the animosity. Taylor did not trust Dave, and she had proven to be, as in Amanda Ripley's excellent book, *High Conflict*,[1] a "conflict entrepreneur" – someone whose stature rises by feeding animosity and pushing others toward deeper conflict. Once the toxin recedes, however, those who have been promoting it often lose credibility.

It was clear to the rest of us that Dave had finally calmed down enough to understand his part in the toxicity and that he needed to listen more deeply to the "why" behind the staff's resistance. It took some time, and a lot of processing, but eventually, as Dave continued to listen to their concerns, the staff felt better able to trust him, and they could focus their efforts on a multitude of ways to become sustainable without severely compromising the mission.

Taylor left her position within two weeks.

If I had known then what I know now, I'd have advised Dave from the beginning to listen with new ears. He was listening primarily for problems that needed solving and for ways to apply his extensive grasp of established business protocol and procedures. These two modes, which I will refer to as Hands and Head listening, are often perceived by our culture as key components in leadership skills. However, without an intention to listen for opportunities to build alliance, grasp larger context, and tune in to the truth beneath the words (Heart listening), the classic perception of "leadership" can only go so far.

Listening exclusively for data and problems to solve will not lead to building empathy and the ability to tune in to another's reality. This requires the ability to excavate conversational layers and uncover the truth beneath the words. This requires intentional Heart listening.

For Dave and many of the rest of us, however, there are significant cultural obstacles that need to be acknowledged before we can amplify our own listening capacity. It's worthwhile to acknowledge what is stacked against us before we begin to discern the listening modalities of Head, Heart, and Hands. That's where we are headed in the next chapter.

# Note

1   *High Conflict*, Ripley, Amanda, 2022

# Obstacles to Listening

## What Gets in the Way . . .

You may have noticed that life has gotten louder. It's not just the din of traffic, the sirens, or the plethora of social media voices all vying for our attention. We have ear buds and headphones and multiple ways to block out what we don't want to pay attention to as we try to focus and make our way through an ever more amplified world. Between our devices, our condensed environments, and a cultural "need for speed", there are significant obstacles to effective listening that are mostly beyond our awareness. But their impact hampers our ability to connect with each other in ways that affect our individual lives, our businesses, and the culture we all share.

## Obstacle 1: Pace of Modern Life – Hamster Wheel in Hyperdrive

The genesis of this book began during the global pandemic. As a result of that calamity, with 80% of my in-person contracts gone up in smoke, I found myself suddenly with lots of time on my hands. By the time you read this, I truly hope the world has recovered from this horrible illness and the resulting economic devastation.

To be honest, I had secretly hoped for a silver lining in the Covid crisis. Once we're forced to slow down, we have, if we choose, an opportunity to stand back from the frenetic hamster wheel so many of us are on. We can then be more discerning about how we prioritize our time once things return to whatever kind of "normal" might emerge.

DOI: 10.4324/9781003296027-3

I discovered for myself, however, that this did not happen. I simply substituted daily life priorities over daily work priorities and still struggled to guard whatever "self care" slots of time I had promised myself. As a culture, many of us were even losing track of what day it was – the "Blursday" phenomenon. Having lived most of my life strapped to my calendar, this was pretty disorienting. A wise friend mused that those less welded to their calendars felt time was going extremely slowly, with the eternally busy people wondering where the day went – whatever day it was. The impact on our listening? For me, I consider my rushed sense of time my most formidable obstacle to good listening, as I am often distracted by the demands of the clock and what I need to do next.

## Obstacle 2: Technology – Trojan Horse or Game Changer?

When I think about it – it's awe-inspiring: just the potential of what we can accomplish as long as we master the tools to get us there. I can set my coffee maker to make coffee by itself at a prescribed time. I can set my alarm so that I get up in time to do the regimen in my exercise app for a precisely chosen amount of time. I can regulate the shower temperature, warm up leftovers for breakfast in the microwave – call up Lyft to get me to an in-person meeting or simply join a zoom call while finishing the last of my coffee . . . and cleaning out my emails . . . catching up on texts . . . and oh, wow! Look at the latest crazy story on Twitter . . . You get the idea. While many of us feel we have mastered the tools of our various technologies, our continual distraction leads to a darker possibility. All that dazzling tech leaves us vulnerable to whomever wants to use our attention to further their own agendas. And it certainly impacts the amount of patience and concentration we have for those trying to speak to us in real time.

## Obstacle 3: "It's All About Me!

Perhaps it started with the Self Help trend and the over 700,000 books currently on the US market within that genre – of which I suppose this book could be considered one. There are just so many ways to improve ourselves, aren't there? It's exhausting. But despite the wisdom in "We cannot change others, we can only change ourselves", our relentless focus *on* ourselves leads to truly poor listening.

I'm going to share a personal story as an example of this. And it saddens me. My mother, according to a rather skewed family dynamic, was considered a good listener. Why? Because she was quiet. No really. That's why. Mom was an introvert's introvert. I sensed her always in the corner somewhere, well-behaved and quiet. But did that mean she was listening? Tuned in? On the same page as whomever she was listening to? And did her listening lead to asking good questions? I remember telling her about my struggles during my late teens – the usual mix – boyfriend fatigue, school is boring, no I *don't* want to live at home during college! Mom would nod her head, murmur sympathetically, often tell me she would pray for me, and then get back to whatever she was doing. When I brought up a specific problem of any kind, her idea of good listening was to offer a similar problem of her own and go on about it. I know she thought we were bonding. But it started to feel like a weird kind of competition to me. So I stopped sharing. For most of the rest of her life, I'm not sure she noticed the banality of our exchanges. But she just couldn't get her focus off herself long enough to ask a question that broke the surface of mundane conversation.

## Obstacle 4: Resistance to Learning and Expertise, "Going With My Gut"

Lifelong learning is very much in our cultural vernacular. Yet I believe that phrase has been applied too often, and pretty exclusively, to retirees – people with time on their hands. That leaves the rest of the adult population doing the best we can with what we already know, digging our mental ruts deeper into our established routines. You may be familiar with the concept of "Fixed" vs. "Growth" mindsets: Carol Dweck[1] established these polar opposite beliefs in regard to learning. Essentially, if we believe our learning capacity is set in stone from birth, regardless of our hard work, we have a "Fixed" mindset. If we believe that we can get smarter with effort and over a lifetime from experiences and exposure to diverse sources, we have a "Growth" mindset. Dweck's research found that those with the later lens scored higher in resiliency and creative thinking. In coaching my clients, I've learned to discern which of these mindsets underlies a client's belief about themselves. Often, they are in the clutches of a Fixed mindset.

I have observed over the years through my work with businesses of many types that highly skilled and educated employees often struggle with a fixed notion of who they are and what they bring to an organization. This entrenchment costs individuals and businesses greatly when interpersonal issues and problems with productivity arise, especially when new learning is required. We saw this dynamic with the staff in Dave's story; the devolving cycle of blame gets triggered by the onset of change, and then the black-and-white, good-and-bad binary sets in.

It could be argued that a fixed mindset and this same accompanying binary have taken hold of American culture. For those working to overcome this toxicity, it requires greater intentionality and a firm commitment to a "Growth" mindset, particularly when we listen to others with different viewpoints, experiences, and status, and most especially when they push our buttons. If I enter into a conversation with my brother-in-law about politics, for example, I'll need to be firm in my quest to learn something in the exchange about the experience that informs his point of view. I'll have to be skillful in asking questions that will get beyond his defenses. And I'll have to look for opportunities to connect rather than simply waiting until he takes a breath and I can inform him of my opinion and how wrong his is.

# Obstacle 5: Reduction in Cultural Empathy

If you are old enough to remember September 11, 2001, with any clarity, you might recall a certain brief but heartening cultural and global reaction – everyone in the world was suddenly focused on Manhattan and the collapse of the World Trade Center. The outpouring of grief and concern across the globe became a tidal wave washing over the nation, cleansing us suddenly of pettier concerns. No matter what the rest of us in other parts of the country may have been going through at the time, it was eclipsed by the agony in New York City, Washington, DC, and rural Pennsylvania.

For many of us who have experienced tragedy and loss, no matter the magnitude, there is an odd kind of silver lining. We are suddenly forced to widen our perspective and clear out whatever smaller concerns we may have been preoccupied with. Our surface priorities are wrenched away, and we are filled with the need to help in whatever way we can.

The only gift in watching my father die was my clear sense of a need to be of service, whether I felt capable or not. Whether my schedule allowed it or not. Whether I could "get along" with the other family members going through their own version of grief – or not.

Over the course of the last decade, our nation has experienced a precipitous drop in the amount of cultural empathy expressed toward others: other nations, other parts of the country, other stories of grief and loss, though the media amplifies them almost to the point of abstraction. It's as if we are contracting our circles of concern to include only those we recognize as similar to ourselves. Without empathy, our ears can only truly listen to those like us in experience, in social status, in tribal identification.

## Obstacle 6: Consumer Choice in Media Consumption

My husband has a habit of tuning in to the Sunday morning news channels – for hours at a time. I can only take so much television because I'm an accomplishment junkie with a To Do list even on a Sunday. Yesterday, as I walked into the living room carrying a load of laundry, I looked up to realize he was listening to a news channel on the opposite end of the spectrum from where he and I usually get our news. I stopped in my tracks. "Really?" I asked. "*That* news channel?" His answer gave me pause. "It's good to tune in to what I don't agree with so I can make sense of why they think this way." He is right, of course, whereas my reaction was more one of feeling as if those same alternative viewpoints might somehow be contagious.

Recent studies on the current state of US politics reveal how Democrats and Republicans are each convinced that if the other side prevails in our culture, it will be the end of our democracy, our way of life, our country as we have known it to be.

In consumer culture, just like Tip O'Neill warned decades ago, we have become convinced that we're entitled not only to our own opinions but to our own facts as well. It becomes ever more difficult to listen to alternative points of view, especially when they come in packaging we don't like. So we continue to listen only to what we already agree with – our fixed mindsets get repeatedly reinforced. Our confirmation biases remain firmly intact.

# Obstacle 7: Confirmation Bias

Warren Buffett, the great financier and savvy observer of human foibles, had this to say about what we do with new facts: "What the human being is best at doing is interpreting all new information so that his/her prior conclusions remain intact."[2] Confirmation bias is not a comfortable subject for any of us who have been on the planet for awhile, largely because we're all guilty of it to one degree or another. In essence, confirmation bias, as Webster's dictionary defines it, is "The tendency to interpret new evidence as confirmation of one's existing beliefs or theories." How does this apply to intentional listening? When we can only hear and retain what already fits with our own firmly held views, we are listening through the lens of confirmation bias. I know that this bias can affect my own learning as well, even when I intentionally apply what I know to be good learning habits. The first information I latch onto almost always aligns with what I already know, as if I'm looking for islands of familiarity in a sea of confusion. This issue gets explored further in relation to the three listening modalities – Head, Heart, and Hands.

# Obstacle 8: Same Old, Same Old

Think back to the last time you had a conversation with a family member. This person is someone you perhaps live with; the rhythms of who they are very familiar: how they think, react, and engage with their world. Did anything they say surprise you? Were you tuned in on a level somewhat deeper than the everyday? Did you learn something you didn't already know?

If we are honest with ourselves, the answer to those questions is probably "No". Why would that be? Is this person simply boring or uninformed or predictable to the point of invisibility? Or are we listening through our own expectancy bias that tends to look for patterns and similarity to what's already known? Marriage counseling often entails encouraging clients to shake up their perceptions of each other – create new experiences, ask deeper questions, be open to surprise in the partner – to listen for different information and emotional authenticity. This active curiosity contains the fundamental belief that we do not, in fact, know everything there is to know about our loved ones. If we intentionally seek delight and surprise, we will listen for new information that can strengthen our bonds and deepen our connections.

# Obstacle 9: Your Ears on Conflict

Think back to the last argument you had with a spouse, co-worker, relative, or perhaps a stranger on the street. How did it go? What did you feel before, during, and after? What were you aware of as tensions heightened, voices grew louder, faces hardened into angry masks? What did you hear? What were you listening for? Were you seeking holes in your opponent's argument? Or were you looking for a way out of the discomfort altogether?

There is no escaping conflict in our lives today. It's everywhere we look: on street corners, in offices, small businesses, online. Countries the world over are steeped in it. Our clients enter their coach sessions primed to pour out the latest heated discussion they had with the important people in their lives and even sometimes with complete strangers.

Conflict causes pain, produces division, reduces productivity everywhere. But it doesn't have to. If we can teach ourselves and our clients to calm down and listen for different clues and apply the 10% rule (each opinion, statement, idea, complaint has at least 10% validity), then we can reap the ultimate benefits of conflict: strengthened bonds, more inclusive decisions, richer authenticity.

How we listen and what we listen for greatly impact our ability to sustain ourselves and our relationships while in the midst of arguments and altercations. Each listening modality has its own tendency to fight, flee, or freeze the intensity of conflict. If we can learn and teach our clients to become aware of these habits, we can begin to transform our significant relationships, our communities, and perhaps, over time, our world.

# Obstacle 10: "Curiosity Is for Kids – Right?"

I am still in disbelief that I actually heard this said in a workshop a few years ago. My mouth may have dropped open, but no one else around me appeared to be stunned. I asked him – I'll call him Adam – to elaborate on that statement, and he named some valid reasons for this belief:

> "Kids are the ones who have time to dig into what intrigues them."
> "It's OK, in fact it's expected that kids are not 'experts' and don't know a whole lot." But this is harder to acknowledge as an adult.
> "I'm so busy trying to build my business, and drill down into those requirements that anything else just feels like distraction."

It's understandable that a focused, driven business person would feel this way. But at some point, people will need to connect with what you're selling or your business will fail. Conveying genuine curiosity is essential to building trust. Trust is at the foundation of a successful client interaction. When I brought that idea into the room, Adam smiled. "Right", he said. "Now you've given me a reason to get curious!"

As a culture, we believe creating true relationships and exhibiting genuine curiosity takes too much time. Maybe so. But it's time well spent.

As to our reluctance to reveal that we don't know something – this is another endemic issue plaguing our learning. It requires vulnerability – when you might have to ask a "stupid" question. You can just imagine the smirks from your highly competitive colleagues. Not happening. No way. But as Brené Brown says "People who wade into discomfort and vulnerability and tell the truth about their stories are the real badasses."[3]

Now here's a question: How will we ever truly keep up with the churn of change in our culture and our world unless we can connect to and communicate our curiosity?

Our lives right now are full of pundits and politicians posing as experts. Where are the good questions? Where are those who are genuinely curious to learn more about navigating through these uncertain times? Where are those who are in touch with, and willing to articulate, what they *don't* know? They are, in fact, everywhere. But we need to be intentional about accessing these voices, and intentional about hearing what they have to say. We may also have to listen in a completely different way, so that we can expand beyond what we already know.

Genuine curiosity is the opposite of fear. You hear that love is the opposite – but in actual experience, love is too big a stretch. All kinds of people can claim they "love" the disabled or Muslims or old hippies, but in that context, the L word is almost meaningless. Genuine curiosity on the other hand, feels much more like love's qualities in action. Curiosity starts from a place of mutual regard: this person's ideas, values, responses are worth eliciting. And it begins with trust: this person will not harm me simply for asking about their experience.

Googling someone is not the same as actually looking them in the eye and asking "How are you – really?" "How do you experience what's happening on our team?" "How do you feel about what she just said?" And truly listening for the answer.

Our resistance to doing this because it takes too much time away from what we have labelled our priorities – is, as mentioned, one of the obstacles to talking through differences or simply encountering each other in a mutually respectful way. Enough of this resistance compounds into a culture and we end up with family fracture, siloed workplaces, and the election season circus that we experience every four years . . . so many of us shocked and awed at all the rage. That degree of anger and blame can only happen when we lose the ability as a country to be curious about the "Other", whatever that term may mean for us.

Think about the last time someone showed genuine curiosity about you or something you were involved in. How did it make you feel to have someone truly slow down enough to ask you a question that demanded more than just a glib, off-the-cuff answer? For me, it happened the other day when meeting a new client. She asked me how I knew I was in a work situation that "fit" me. I had to slow down and visualize the components of that workplace before answering, and my response surprised us both: congruent body language, facial messaging and . . . genuine curiosity in grappling with the dynamics of diversity and change. Suddenly, we understood each other more deeply.

Curiosity is defined as: 1. "the desire to learn or know more about something or someone", or 2. "something that is interesting because it is unusual." The Curiosity Quotient is a term coined by Thomas Friedman and broken down into the Curiosity Values. You can hunt and peck around, as I did, for an actual "Curiosity Quiz".[4] I took it, and it was revealing to see how so many of our daily habits and rituals are determined by how much curiosity we possess.

In the coming chapters, the importance of curiosity, and what each modality is genuinely curious about – will give you additional information about your own listening tendencies as well as those of your clients. You'll get an even better idea once you take the quiz in Section 5.

Now, welcome to the Listening Modalities: Head, Heart, and Hands.

# Notes

1    "Carol Dweck Revisits the 'Growth Mindset", Dweck, Carol, *Education Week*, 2015
2    "Tackling the Confirmation Bias Beast", Annotti, Joe, *TVNewsCheck*, 2022
3    *Rising Strong: The Reckoning. The Rumble. The Revolution*, Brown, Brené 2019
4    *Assessment: What's Your Curiosity Profile?* https://hbr.org/2015/12/assessment-whats-your-curiosity-profile, Harvard Business Review, 2015

# Listening Styles: Head Listening – Just the Facts Ma'am

## HEAD LISTENING MODALITY:

### SECTION SUMMARY

**Head Listeners Are Challenged To:**

- Hear & retain unspoken interpersonal information
- Stay engaged in emotional conversations
- Identify and own their unconscious biases

**Head Listeners Listen for:**

- **Rational function:** Facts, numbers, anything that can be measured
- **The Known:** Established patterns, what's been proven to be true
- **Timeframe:** The past

**Head Listener Professions and Industries:**
(Not a complete list)

- Data Analysis • Engineering Computer Programming • STEM Education • Science and Research Insurance Adjustment • Securities and Investments • Cybersecurity • Corporate Leadership • Military Leadership • Library Science • Historical Research • Aeronautics Medical Research and Technology

**Head Listeners Are Curious About...**

- How something works
- Linear progressions
- The factual truth: What, where, when, & how

### POSITIVE INTELLIGENCE CROSSOVER

### Benefits & Challenges

**Head Listening Provides:**

- Rational balance
- Fact-driven input in emotionally charged situations
- Solidly researched and retained grasp of information
- A rational challenge to confirmation bias
- Emotional detachment to gain perspective

**Saboteurs**

- **Hyper Rational:** Intense focus on rational processing of experience, including relationships, can present as unfeeling, arrogant, and uncaring
- **Stickler:** Perfectionist, extreme need for order & organization

**Sage Powers**

- **Explore:** The ability to seek out facts and undergo thorough research
- **Navigate:** Alignment with values, priorities, vision, and a wider perspective

# Todd's Story: The Game is Key . . .

"Todd" is in his late 30s, currently single, an engineer employed at a major tech firm for about five years, and newly promoted to a managerial position within the department he had been working with throughout his tenure at the company. He's a highly skilled and competent employee of Asian heritage. He came to me for coaching as a way to help him "fit in" with his colleagues at work, given his new role.

Cultural "fit" is complex. Many HR departments try to fix complexity with the same rule structures and procedures that address complicated problems like fairness and benefits. But complex problems arise from human behavior and human complexity. There are many factors at play, not all of them straightforward. From listening to Todd explain his discomfort with his colleagues, I could discern confusion in how he was processing his interactions. I gave him the listening assessment, and the results were no surprise: Todd was a strong Head listener.

*Head Listeners Listen for:*
- Rational function: Facts, numbers, anything that can be measured
- The known: Established patterns, what's been proven to be true
- Timeframe: The past

*Head Listeners Are Curious About . . .*
- How something works
- Linear progressions
- The factual truth: "What, where, when, and how"

DOI: 10.4324/9781003296027-5

Todd relayed his analysis of the problem: other people seemed to get along better with each other, and he felt left out and uncomfortable around some of the more gregarious interactions. Though he had more tenure in this company than many of his colleagues, his seniority didn't help him feel comfortable, in fact, he felt it might have been even more of a barrier. He was also starting to wonder if his race was a factor.

When I asked him to share what others talked about in the lunchroom or on coffee breaks, Todd was pretty vague and seemed a bit bored: sports, kids, "whatever's on Netflix". His interactions with those that surrounded him were strictly confined to the work at hand.

Next, I asked Todd how he spent his leisure time – what he did for fun. He took this as an odd question, and asked for some clarity as to how his activities away from work had any relevance to his fitting in with colleagues. I found his pushback to this question to be interesting. Eventually, he revealed that he had been a Dungeons and Dragons[1] devotee for several years, and he had a lively group online that he engaged with on weekends. He had not shared this information with anyone at work, fearing that people would think he was "weird". Todd's current experience had very clear boundaries between work life and leisure time.

There is a reference in the Positive Intelligence[2] program developed by Shirzad Chamine to this kind of compartmentalization. Chamine, an engineer by training, sorts our perception into two channels working together simultaneously: the Data channel; facts, information, what is already proven, known and relevant to the topic at hand. This channel is clearly in the realm of Head listening and where Todd felt most comfortable. Then there is Chamine's "PQ channel", where other kinds of information are located: body language, facial expression, vocal tone – indicators of the truth beneath the content and, in the framework I've developed, clearly aligned with Heart listening. Todd's habitual focus on Data channel information was, I suspected, preventing him from tuning in to other kinds of signals that would allow him to find opportunities to connect with colleagues.

We are not, after all, cogs in a mechanical system. Every situation offers us information on a number of channels if we can tune in to them. Todd's Head listening had served him very well in his career: he was suited to work he enjoyed. He was thriving professionally within a very structured organization, and he would have multiple opportunities to advance.

Exclusive reliance on Head listening, however, is lonely, and the young man seated in front of me was, though he struggled to admit it, suffering from loneliness.

In addition, while this modality is highly prized in most corporate settings, Head listening is not always what we most need in the face of sudden change, whether positive, as was Todd's promotion, or unwelcome.

James Pennebaker, a professor in social psychology at Southern Methodist University in Texas, led an intriguing study with 63 engineers that had recently lost their jobs.[3] The study was designed to find out if writing about emotions would help some of these engineers to regain employment. Pennebaker divided the group into thirds, where one group would focus on in-depth journalling about their emotions; a second group would write about ordinary, non-emotional topics; and a third group would do no writing at all. After four months' time, the study had to come to a halt, as most of the engineers in the emotional writing group had gotten new jobs.

I got curious about Todd's D&D experience, and I asked him to tell me more about it. He began to answer me with granular details about how the games are structured, so I invited him to pause for a second. I needed to clarify my question.

"I'd like to know what it is about Dungeons and Dragons that intrigues you so much." Todd looked confused for a second, then answered with "I don't know, I guess I like coming up with storylines and characters. I get to use my imagination in new ways." I noticed a shift in tone as Todd answered me; I felt he was starting to open up, so I moved on to my next question. "Todd, how does engaging with this game make you feel?" Todd's face went blank. He shifted uncomfortably in his seat. "I don't know, uhm, maybe . . . happy I guess? Curious about what people come up with? Is that what you mean?"

Yes! That was a beginning. Todd got through his initial discomfort with the subject and revealed he had been with this online group for over a decade. Some of the members had been childhood friends, and he felt like he could be at his most relaxed and authentic in their company. He also admitted that yes, engaging online felt much more comfortable than having to talk to people in person. As Todd's workplace adapts to a post-COVID world and moves from the strictly virtual into more hybrid interactions, Todd finds himself feeling increasingly uncomfortable.

I let him know that part of our work together would involve bridging his two worlds, his workplace and his online game life, so that he might be able to access more relaxed authenticity in his work environment, which could also create pathways to friendship.

## The Coach's Perspective: Questions and Applications

1. What elements of Todd's situation would you first address as his coach?
2. What factors are standing in his way in making friendlier connections with his colleagues?
3. What changes would you suggest specific to Todd's listening habits?
4. How might you use Todd's Dungeons & Dragons experience as a coaching tool?

## You Might Try This: Make It a Game

If you have a client with a strong Head modality but who struggles to connect with others in satisfying ways, consider this suggestion:

> Of the three modalities, Head listeners feel the most comfortable with structure and rules. Todd had found he could enjoy using his imagination within the invented D&D world of clear rules and boundaries. Could you devise for your client a "game" with clear rules of engagement built on appropriate challenges? For example: I suggested to Todd that he experiment with tuning in to another's emotions (Heart listening) and naming those feelings in a low-stakes setting. I asked him to try this in three different places, with three different strangers, between our appointments.

Todd was instructed to do the following: When he was next in the grocery store, or a similar errand-oriented place, as he stood in line to pay, he was to focus on the person taking his payment. He would take in their posture, facial expressions, tone of voice, and attitude towards those in line, and from these signals, make a guess as to the person's emotional state. Could he "read" how the clerk's day had gone so far? What signals was he picking up? Finally, Todd had one remaining challenge for at least one of the three encounters: he was to say something to the cashier, like "You seem a bit tired, have you had a tough day?" Or, "It's nice to see a smiling face this morning, I hope the rest of your day goes well too." My reason for this assignment: If Todd could take the time to practice tuning in to another's emotional state when in fairly low-stakes situations, he would become more adept at the skill in reading his co-workers and those he supervised.

Though he was at first resistant to this exercise, once I explained the possible benefits to his work relationships, Todd agreed to try. I encouraged him to have a little fun with this, to think of it as a game, and to that end, we designed a point system for the exercise:

Todd would get at least 2 points each time he attempted to take in another's emotional state, 5 points for naming the feeling out loud, with an extra 3 points if the person's response was positive.

I felt Todd's energy shift once the challenge was presented in game form with clear rules. At our next session, he was very excited to share his points: 25 out of a possible 30! Even more than the point tallies, I could see that Todd was on his way to creating better relationships in his work environment. Once he could connect with others emotionally, Todd would be better able to build trust and perhaps enjoy some beneficial workplace friendships – even offline – just by learning to listen differently and tuning in to new information.

## You Might Try This: What Am I Missing?

There is a meditation exercise I sometimes begin a session with, part of which applies directly to listening. I call it the 3-2-1 method, and it may sound familiar to you. Ask your client to take a few deep breaths and focus on three things they can see. Ask them to try to eliminate whatever else might be there to see so that visual attention is tuned only to those three items. Ask them to take a deep breath, close their eyes, and focus on three things they can hear. Encourage them to tune in to subtle sounds in the room, underneath the louder stimuli. Then ask for another deep breath and focus on three physical sensations. The rest of the exercise involves attention on two things to see, hear, and feel, and then one thing. By the end of the activity, time has slowed down and attention is better focused. You can see how listening for what is underneath the more obvious sounds can be a challenge but also develops skill in more attentive listening in a variety of situations.

## Notes

1   Dungeons and Dragons: https://dnd.wizards.com/
2   Positive Intelligence: www.positiveintelligence.com/
3   "Expressive Writing and Coping with Job Loss", Pennebaker, James, *JSTOR*, 1994

# Gretchen's Story – It's Not Just the Content . . .

"Gretchen" had just been promoted to vice president of communications at a statewide credit union network. To this point, she had held a position as head of information technology for almost five years. During that time, she impressed many with her ability to recall the specific details of a client's IT history and the granular processes involved in those particular situations. Highly introverted, Gretchen passed up most opportunities to put herself in the spotlight. At sometimes fractious meetings, however, hers was the trusted voice of reason, clarity, and calm that could get her team back on track with her grasp of company history, accurate data recall, and grounded interpretation of the facts. When the VP position came open, and the management team was asked who they trusted the most in their daily departmental interactions, everyone mentioned Gretchen's name. Ultimately, the position went to Gretchen over a field of highly charismatic and experienced contenders. Why? She had demonstrated quiet, competent, fact-focused leadership. The company trusted her.

Many of us have friends and colleagues who can rattle off facts and statistics at any time. Their power of recall seems endless. They're the ones with the calm quizzical faces in a heated discussion, and their input can re-focus the entire group on what's already known, proven, time-tested. You know when you talk with a Head listener: they remember exactly the concrete elements of your interaction. They can be the voice of calm that elicits respect and trust. As we've seen with Gretchen and Todd and with Dave in the first chapter, those who have this kind of listening and content recall are highly prized professionally and are often placed in positions of leadership.

DOI: 10.4324/9781003296027-6

STEM occupations and industries are filled with Head listeners. This modality thrives on more data, content, granular procedures, plotting, and mapping points A to Z. They are scientists looking for proof, investigative journalists looking for the truth, leaders steering a course toward the tried and true. In addition, as illustrated in the next story, this kind of listening can often be the antidote for confirmation bias.

I worked with Gretchen on her speaking and professional presence. As a skilled and valued employee newly promoted to vice president, she suddenly felt she was in the "hot seat" in a position that demanded higher visibility. In her former role, as part of a team, she was responsible for content creation, data research, and making sure the team's information was rock solid. But having to engage listeners in her topic? Taking the temperature of the audience and adjusting her message accordingly? Finding the story that could bring the numbers to life? Suddenly, this highly competent and capable woman felt like she was all thumbs.

"I don't think I've had to make a single solo presentation since defending my thesis in grad school." Gretchen recalled in our initial session. "And even then, I thought of that as something I just had to endure."

"Do you remember what you did to prepare for that presentation?" I asked.

"Just memorized everything as best I could and hoped people were looking at the slides instead of at me." Then she added, tilting her chin up a bit "My slides were always excellent." I smiled. This was Gretchen's way of letting me know that even if her delivery was rocky, the content was off-the-charts terrific. I had no doubt.

"Do you remember the impact you had on your listeners?" I asked.

Gretchen laughed. "I remember that my thesis was accepted!"

We both laughed. "Fair enough" I said. "And now the criteria for an impactful presentation has changed. It requires deeper listener engagement."

As we continued our sessions, we focused on finding ways that Gretchen could better connect with her listeners. I could tell she had worked extremely hard on the assignments I gave her – in fact, I began to feel she was working a bit too hard. After our third or fourth session, Gretchen made an admission.

"I feel a little like an imposter in this role," Gretchen said flatly at the start of our fourth session.

I was surprised, and aware that perhaps Gretchen's struggle with public speaking was rooted more deeply, which is very common for many of my clients.

"Gretchen, I'm sorry to hear that, coming from someone with such a high degree of competence. Can you say more about what triggers that feeling?"

"Well, I did the marketing summary presentation last week." She took a deep breath and was silent for a moment. I feared the worst. This had been an important session with many VIPs in the room. She looked at me, dropped her eyes, and shrugged.

"Oh, it went fine, I guess. At least Mitch and President Freeman said 'Nice presentation' to me when it was finished."

"And how did that make you feel?"

She looked down at her hands clasped in her lap.

"Okay, I guess. But it was really Jen and William's summary that clinched the session."

I could tell that Gretchen's anxiety was causing her to hear the encouragement of her male superiors – statements like "Nice presentation" as verbal pats on the head and evidence that she was not measuring up to the demands of her position. Additionally, I noticed that she often credited others involved in her presentations for the success of the efforts overall. Here she was doing it again.

Gill Corkindale, in an HBR article titled "Overcoming Imposter Syndrome",[1] highlights some toxic internal beliefs that fuel the problem:

**"I must not fail"** This internal message brings enormous pressure and makes it impossible to enjoy success with increased responsibility and visibility. With this belief, Gretchen can't fail, or she will be "found out".

**"I feel like a fake"** Gretchen believed she could often give the impression of competency but still struggled with doubts that she deserved her promotion.

**"It's all down to luck"** Very few white males seem to harbor this belief, but for others, Gretchen among them, the tendency to attribute success at work to colleagues, good timing, or "luck" is, over time, problematic in owning and building on one's success.

**"Success is no big deal"** Continually discounting one's success and the tendency to deflect compliments are hallmarks of Imposter Phenomenon. After awhile, even those who feel drawn to acknowledge Gretchen's excellent work may refrain from doing so.

Do any of your clients suffer from this kind of twisted logic? These phrases often enter into conversations with my highly professional female clients, and I myself have suffered from these toxic patterns as well. How might intentional listening help improve this experience?

As a primary Head listener, Gretchen is most comfortable in the realm of concrete knowledge, proven facts, data, and numbers. But now, other skills are called for. Anytime we, as successful adults, are asked to operate out of our familiar skillset, there will be a degree of feeling like an imposter. The issue in Gretchen's case, I believe, was one of judging that feeling as bad and wrong.

Think back to childhood, or remember your own children in their early years. Children learn about other's experiences: astronaut, doctor, ballet dancer, by playing pretend. They step into a role so that they can better see themselves in it. They listen for cues for how to be and what to do. If I could get Gretchen to listen for how effective speakers engage their audience, their vocal tone, the stories they use, their interaction with the audience, *without getting distracted by the content*, and then get her to practice those new elements with me as a way of "trying on" a new speaker personae, it might be possible for Gretchen to become more comfortable stepping into this requirement in her new role.

I decided on a multi-pronged strategy to help Gretchen experience herself as a successful presenter. First, she needed to observe and listen for information that, as a solid Head listener, had escaped her attention prior to our work together. As you know by now, Head listeners are primarily, and often exclusively, tuned in to facts, data, and content while missing the critical information underneath the words: body language, vocal tone, facial expression, and so on. Gretchen's initial assignments included a series of TED talks on subjects she was not particularly interested in. Why? For this first task, I needed to get her focused on the "how" rather than the "what" of a presentation, and I wanted content that would not prove distracting to her.

As you might expect, Gretchen was initially rather irritated by having to watch speakers talking about fashion, water systems, and permaculture.

"Really?" She asked once I laid out the topic choices. "I have to make time to watch people talk about something I'm not remotely interested in?"

I rose to the challenge. "Gretchen, your learning right now has nothing to do with content. As a skilled Head listener, content is your A game. But I want you to pay attention to *how* the content is delivered, *not* the content itself." Once I broke down the elements of what I wanted her to pay attention to: vocal tone, body language, gestures, she understood what I was after.

"I would also like you to assess the speaker's impact on your own sensibilities: how did this person make you feel? What might they be trying to cause in the listener? How, specifically, do they go about that?"

"Eeek," she responded, but there was a smile on her face.

I continued. "And Gretchen, this is important. What tools do you see that you would consider experimenting with in your own presentations?"

Once I could get Gretchen to agree to "try on" new behavior and communication elements in her speeches, I could add more of them in for subsequent sessions.

Gretchen taught me that Head listeners, as do many of the rest of us, appreciate a specific detailed breakdown and justification for assignments. I was happy to provide them. You'll find some of these tools in the following sections, but first, some questions for you to consider.

## The Coach's Perspective: Questions and Applications

1. Which of Gretchen's issues would you address first, and why?
2. How do Gretchen's listening habits affect those issues?
3. How might you structure Gretchen's assignments so she can improve her listening habits?

## You Might Try This . . . The Vocal Detective

I have spent quite a few years digging into the impact of voice quality on perception and learning. Because Gretchen needed clear structure in building her listening skills in modalities other than Head listening, I had her become aware of the difference in impact on listeners between the emphasis of vowels vs. emphasized consonants.[2]

Pay attention to your vocal tone next time you speak to a loved one who lives with you and contrast your voice with the one you use with a colleague. We tend to stress and extend our vowels with people we feel most comfortable with, and we are more "formal", stressing our consonants, in professional situations.

Here's another example: If you are a parent of a small child, or if you have a pet you are fond of, notice how many extended vowels you use to get their attention focused on something. Chances are you will use a wider range of high and lower pitches, and also you most likely will extend the vowels you use in an attempt to engage them. And if you are a parent of a teenager – getting their attention is very different. I noticed with my teenage daughter that I often needed to raise the volume of my voice and stress the consonants, especially if I was giving a direction I needed her to pay attention to in order to keep her safe. I use a painting analogy here of the consonants as the pencil line drawing – the clear boundaries between black and white space, objects, shapes. Vowels then, provide the color – the emotional texture, the "mood" of the painting, the sensual engagement.

Once Gretchen started to get curious about this vowel/consonant distinction, she began experimenting. Stressing vowels in the stories added emotional color to the statistics in her presentations, and clearly stressing her consonants energized her game plans for moving forward. She admitted to me in one of her last sessions that she was actually starting to have fun! Once a client can begin to get curious and even enjoy themselves in a task . . . the Imposter problem seems to dissipate.

## You Might Try This . . . Listen for Something New

It can be fascinating to discover what we notice, and listen to, in unfamiliar places. I've asked clients to begin noticing, when they travel to a new country, what they attach their attention to first. How do we make the unfamiliar familiar? And how do our listening modalities help or hinder that progress? If, for example, you invite a Head listening client to go somewhere unfamiliar to them for an hour: a new town or neighborhood or a walk in the woods, ask them to write down two or three things that they hear. This is purely observational, without assigned listening of any kind. After a week's tracking, see if you can both discern patterns in their listening.

## Notes

1   "Overcoming Imposter Syndrome", Corkindale, Gill, *Harvard Business Review*, 2008
2   *Persuasion and Influence for Dummies*, page 309, Kuhnke, Elizabeth, Wiley & Sons, 2012

# Gabe's Story . . . No Joy on the Dean's List

Gabe connected with me when he was about to begin his junior year at a highly prestigious college in our area. He was gifted in the STEM subjects, such that he was already being recruited for positions in information technology and cybersecurity with global corporations.

"And I'm not even out of school yet!" he exclaimed, slouching in his chair and shaking his head.

Gabe is a slight young man with dark red curly hair, sad brown eyes, and a goatee struggling to be born. He was dressed in the casual jeans-and-hoodie uniform of a Gen Z techie. The sweatshirt proclaimed "Skip a Straw – Save a Turtle!"

The recruitment news might have excited another student and been taken as an indication that they were on the right track, but Gabe looked absolutely stressed and miserable. I knew, from a rather panicked email his mother had sent me, that Gabe had considered dropping out of school altogether. I also knew that I was somehow expected to make sure he did no such thing.

Yet there was no disputing the misery emanating from the young man in front of me.

"Gabe, let's start at the beginning here." I watched him sit up a bit straighter. "How did you feel when you began your freshman year?"

Gabe went back to shrugging. "Okay, I guess."

"And was the Digital and Computational Studies program the reason you chose this school?"

"I guess." He shrugged again. "But mostly it was the full ride they gave me." He looked out the window. "My parents don't have a ton of money, so it was a no-brainer."

DOI: 10.4324/9781003296027-7

We talked some more about his school experience. Gabe found the scholastic demands of the competitive program he was in as "kind of interesting, I guess", and his professors "OK, I guess", but the rigors of a multi-class schedule were "really stressful – everything has to be so perfect, and I can't always get stuff done on time". His mother had mentioned a problem with procrastination and time management in her email, but I was more interested in Gabe's stated demand for perfection.

"Tell me more about 'everything needing to be perfect', Gabe."

He looked at me like I had just proven myself an imbecile. "Uhmmm. It's like . . . everywhere? TikTok, Instagram, the profs, the parents, employers, you name it. Got a test? You have to ace it. Got an interview for a job? You need to be their number one choice. Got a girlfriend? She better be a supermodel – I mean . . . it's relentless!"

"That sounds awful, Gabe, really." There was silence for a beat or two. Then I asked, "What do you do to relax?"

He gave a disgusted snort. "Watch Netflix – just like everyone else."

"Do you ever have a chance to get outside? Play sports or anything like that?"

"No time. Gotta study." He paused, and an almost wistful expression crossed his face. "And, like, I used to play soccer. But to play soccer at school now – you can't just do it to have fun right? You have to make practices and drills and games and you have to up your skills and . . . then it's just f*cking work like everything else!"

You might recognize Gabe as typical of a generation with particularly high rates of stress, often due to the relentless ubiquity of social media, along with the demands of a competitive and intensely materialistic culture. Both of these influences reflect highly unreasonable expectations of human beings. And they amplify the toxic impact of perfectionism.

A study published in the American Psychological Association's *Psychological Bulletin* attempts to bring some clarity to the impact of perfectionism on college students. "Perfectionism Is Increasing Over Time: A Meta-Analysis of Birth Cohort Differences From 1989 to 2016" by Thomas Curran and Andrew P. Hill[1] introduced the term "multidimensional perfectionism". The authors unpack this concept into three components: self-oriented perfectionism (expectations of perfecting oneself), socially prescribed perfectionism (perceived perfection demands from social media and the surrounding culture), and other-oriented perfectionism (perfection demanded of others). The study concluded that rates of perfectionism, in all three categories, but particularly with socially prescribed perfectionism, have increased substantially over the course of 25 years.

Gabe described an experience all too common in his generation, but it can be particularly acute in Head listeners. When I gave him both the Listening Styles and Positive Intelligence assessments, Gabe scored very high as a Head listener, and his primary saboteurs appeared to be Hyperrational, Stickler, and Controller. No wonder perfectionism was hammering at him, from the outside and within.

Because Head listeners are so tuned in to facts and data: what is proven as accurate, proven to be the "best", the conclusions they draw about themselves, their circumstances, and those around them can be very concrete: good/bad, black/white, right/wrong. There is little room for nuance in a worldview like this, and it can be extraordinarily punishing towards oneself and others.

I have found summarizing to be a good tool when interacting with a Head listener.

"Alright Gabe, just so we can get on the same page, tell me if I'm getting an accurate picture here." He sat up again, and shifted himself into a somewhat more alert slouch.

"I'm seeing a smart talented guy who has worked extremely hard for the first two years of college but is under enormous pressure to succeed. I'm guessing some of this pressure is sourced in our culture, some of it from your parents, and some of it self induced. Am I right so far?"

Gabe sat up a bit straighter. "I don't know about the self-induced part."

"Really, Gabe?" I found his pushback interesting and worth a little pushback of my own. "It would be highly unusual for anyone in our culture, but particularly someone your age, to have escaped internalizing super-high expectations of yourself.

He shrugged. "I guess." Back to slouching.

"Here's the thing, Gabe. We can't do much about what those around us say and do. We can't do much about the messages from media and culture and all the rest of it. But we can do something about our own response to it. We can set boundaries against toxic messaging. And we can prioritize our own emotional health. We can put impossibly high expectations that are beamed at us from all these sources into perspective. And to your credit, Gabe, I think you are already starting to do this."

I watched his face get quizzical. "What do you mean?" he said. "All I did was come to this appointment".

I smiled. "Exactly."

Over the next four months, I continued to work with Gabe on identifying perfectionistic demands before they took hold of him. We concentrated on ways he could strengthen his mental fitness muscles through regular and consistent mindfulness activities, journalling, and intentionally dismantling his internal judge.

I happen to be a strong believer in the power of nature to restore sanity, but as a Head listener-hyper-rational-STEM kind of guy, Gabe was very much not. So, after a few weeks of his resistance, I understood his need for solid proof to determine the value of anything we might do together. I assigned him a book to read: *Nature Fix* by Florence Williams, a scientist and researcher on a mission to prove irrefutably and with solid data the restorative power of nature on the human psyche. Once he had data-backed proof of value, Gabe started to take his "nature fix" assignments more seriously – even digging into specific biological questions and applications on his own, without my prompting.

I'm glad to report that Gabe stayed in school. And he switched his degree focus to include biology and ocean robotics.

As with many of us, Gabe will battle toxic messages around perfectionism for much of his adult life. But now he has some tools. Now he can better honor and tune in to his internal truths to minimize the stress caused from outside forces.

I ran into his mother at the farmer's market recently. She was happy to report that Gabe has a new girlfriend. She's not a supermodel. She's a law student focused on climate change and sustainability.

# The Coach's Perspective: Questions and Applications

1. How does perfectionism impact your clients' self esteem, relationships, and professional life?
2. Regarding your clients who struggle with perfectionism, which of the three dimensions: self-oriented, socially prescribed, or other-oriented, afflict them the most?

3. In your experience, do you find differences in degrees of perfection-ism in socioeconomic status, gender, age, or race?
4. Perfectionism can be particularly difficult for Head listeners, as there is oftentimes a very rigid standard of what is acceptable or not. How might you help your Head listener clients put themselves and their actions in a healthier perspective?

## You Might Try This . . . The Time Box

This can be an effective tool, as it gives the client total and complete permission to experience the power of their own internal negative judge-ments and emotions – for a very defined period of time. This can be dif-ficult to do at first with Head listeners, as they tend to downplay the strength of their emotions. But once they can embrace the requirements: to voice their negative thoughts aloud and uncensored for five to ten min-utes (or whatever time limit you have determined will be appropriate to the client's needs), they are often startled by the toxicity and veracity of their own internal messaging. This may provide the proof they need to undertake the work of dismantling these influences.

Within the Positive Intelligence Model, one of the starting exercises asks participants to embody and voice the negative messaging of their internal critic. I invite clients, after they've experienced the vitriol of this entity, to begin to have some fun with it. For instance, my internal critic has a name: Aunt Eunice. She has a dyed-black bubble-cut hairdo, a very nasal voice, a cigarette holder, and a large martini glass filled with her favorite alcoholic beverage. When I've had enough of her sideswiping negativity, I thank her for her input, for trying to keep me safe, and I invite her to refresh her martini in the third basement of the Kym's Head hotel. Once I can laugh at her, Aunt Eunice loses her power over me.

## You Might Try This . . . Expand the Perspective

Perfectionism can cause clients to overgeneralize and rigidly define them-selves, their experiences, or those they are connected to in a very nega-tive way. The Positive Intelligence model offers five distinct Sage powers to counter the influence of our internal judge and saboteurs. One of them, the Navigator power, is all about expanding our perspective to include a wider range of considerations. For example, when Gabe came into his session complaining about a testy interaction with a professor or fellow student, I might counter with; "Well Gabe, how often does this happen with _____? When was the last time you had a difficult conversation with them? If you could take a measure of all the times you've engaged with this person – what would your aggregate assessment be?" Unless the relationship is truly veering toward problematic, the aggregate score is almost always an improvement over the initial emotional assessment.

# Note

1    "Perfectionism Is Increasing Over Time: A Meta-Analysis of Birth Cohort Differences From 1989 to 2016", Curran, Thomas and Hill, Andrew P., *APA PsycNet*, 2019; *Nature Fix*, 2018

# Theresa's Story . . . Do You Hear What I Hear?

"Theresa" was a young, newly hired communications associate in a high-profile organization. She was an excellent researcher and writer, skills that positioned her well in her role. Within six weeks, however, it became clear that Theresa was having trouble adjusting to her new job. She had difficulty processing her emotions in a professional setting, and her unpredictability, demonstrated as either shutting down or blowing up, was impacting her team's morale. The executive director felt that she could use some help in her interpersonal communications.

I've placed Theresa's story here as an inverse example of how Head listening can help modulate certain kinds of biases. Theresa was a primary Hands listener, with Head listening as a secondary modality, which served her well in the research aspects of her job. As we saw with Gretchen, Head listeners can employ a degree of focus and emotional detachment in work-related interactions. But Theresa was not utilizing these skills in her interpersonal listening.

In my first interview with Theresa as her coach, I found her to be personable but guarded about her experience on the job. I assured her that I was hired to assist her in what appeared to be a rocky tenure so far and that everything she told me would be confidential unless she specifically wanted me to share it. Once our boundaries became clear, she agreed to continue meeting with me.

Theresa began by complaining that she felt "forced" to participate in team meetings and suspected that the rest of the team had something against her.

"I don't get why these meetings are mandatory. And there's so many of them! They feel like a waste of time to me." Theresa rolled her eyes and

DOI: 10.4324/9781003296027-8

shifted in her seat, as if signaling that she felt the same way about our session. It was time to deepen the exchange.

"Tell me more about why they feel like a waste of time."

She took a deep breath, sighed, and closed her eyes, as if she were resigned to my exasperating questions.

"Nothing gets done! I mean, I can see that other people enjoy these meetings, I just don't." Theresa shifted in her chair again and looked at her watch. Tempted as I was to smile at her impatience (fairly characteristic for a Hands listener), I was about to annoy her further.

"Why do you think the others enjoy these meetings?"

Theresa looked at the ceiling and said, "Well, they all know each other and they all seem to get along."

"So it feels more like a social gathering to you?"

"Yeah, exactly!" "Like I said, a waste of time."

I tried another tack.

"So there you are, in this mandatory meeting, seeing other people talking and having a good time. You are feeling impatient and irritated, and you just want to get back to your own work, do I have this right?"

Theresa nodded her head vigorously, and answered, "Yup," with special emphasis on the final "p".

"So Theresa – why do you think you were asked to attend this meeting?"

"Exactly my question!" She looked directly at me for the first time in our session. "Why?!"

"In fact," she continued, "I don't know why I'm here talking to you. I mean, no offense, but I feel like you're supposed to turn me into a more sociable person, and monitor me or something."

Yes! Some engaged authenticity. Now, we were getting somewhere.

I reminded Theresa that I had been hired to assist her, which she could choose to interpret not as my "monitoring" her but as evidence of the organization's investment in her success. "In fact," I began, "You could choose to consider the mandatory meetings an attempt by the executive director to have the others get to know you better, and vice versa."

"Well, it's not working." Theresa crossed her arms defiantly, but the angle of her shoulders revealed a sadness she had not displayed until now.

"Theresa, you said earlier that you felt as if the rest of the team had something against you. Could you say more about that?"

She squirmed in her seat. Surprisingly, she couldn't really point to anything specific that had occurred but nonetheless claimed that she "just knew" that the rest of the team didn't like her. Continued questions revealed that in her prior job, which Theresa had very much enjoyed, she had been laid off with no warning. Later on, it was made clear to her through other channels that she had lost her job due not just to budget cuts but because her supervisor felt she did not fit in well with the company culture. The impact of this news had a devastating effect on her.

"I had no idea that I wasn't fitting in. I mean, I didn't really think about it. I'm an introvert, and there were a lot of talkers in that place, but I did an excellent job there. I don't get why fitting in is so important. Now it's happening all over again!"

I saw now that there was history behind Theresa's tension, and I thanked her for sharing it with me. While I understood and empathized with her fear that similar factors in her current job would lead to her being laid off, I knew that her defensive negativity needed to be dismantled.

One of the primary tenets of the Positive Intelligence model[1] is the understanding that negative encounters, particularly when they are repeated, present us with gifts and opportunities for learning and growth. If Theresa could begin to consider these meetings a way to connect positively with her teammates, her negative expectations would begin to shift. However, she would have to start intentionally listening for positive potential rather than reinforcement of prior negative experience. This would not be easy.

You may have encountered clients and colleagues with Theresa's defensiveness. They can often be labelled "glass half-empty" people by colleagues and co-workers. Theresa had a strong negative bias, one partially built from previous work experience but now being actively reinforced in her current position. Remember our definition of confirmation bias: "The tendency to interpret new evidence as confirmation of one's existing beliefs or theories."

Kate Murphy, author of You're Not Listening,[2] coined the term "expectancy bias" which serves to fill our very human need for order and consistency. As we try to make sense of unfamiliar territory, we actively seek to turn the unknown into the known, perhaps especially when impacted by negative prior experience. In our mental "storage closet", we put people and situations into boxes with labels in order to make ourselves feel safe. These labels can be created by cultural stereotypes or simply based on one's personal experience. According to Murphy, "The irony is that by remaining defensive and not listening fully, you actually increase your chances of responding inappropriately or insensitively." This had certainly been happening with Theresa. In our weekly sessions, I found myself working diligently to "translate" actions and protocols that had put her on defense in order to offer more positive interpretations of others' words and behaviors.

It was clear to me that Theresa needed to widen her perspective in her interpersonal work encounters, to actively listen for and make note of positive exchanges, and, if possible, learn to "assume positive intent"[3] on the part of others. Easier said than done.

In research on social connection and the barriers that inhibit it, in an article titled "The Liking Gap in Groups and Teams",[4] Erica Boothby and her colleagues coin a deceptively simple term – the "Liking Gap". The team got curious about our under- or overestimations about how much other people like us. They found that, in general, the research revealed that people tend to come off better in initial conversations with groups or individuals than they think they do; in other words, the "liking gap" is largely in our own minds. But the extent to which it takes hold and becomes an underlying belief can greatly impact job satisfaction. This was clearly the case with Theresa.

In one of our early sessions, Theresa entered the room, sat down hard and announced, "I'm getting close to quitting this job!"

I was startled. I felt we had made some progress in her last session, as she understood the need to take a deep breath, assume positive intent, and apply intentional listening in order to interpret her interactions more positively.

"What happened, Theresa?" I also knew by now that the dramatic announcement was an attempt to cover her insecurity and confusion. She went on to describe another team meeting.

"Every time I put forward an idea, someone had a reason it couldn't be implemented! After awhile I just shut up."

"That sounds awful, Theresa. I'm sorry you came away feeling shut down. Can I ask you a few questions about your experience?

She shrugged despondently. "I guess".

"What did you listen for in this meeting?"

"Oh right." I had suggested in our last session that she begin noticing how others substantiated their ideas: the language and vernacular they used, whether there might be some verbal shorthands between them, and how often Theresa felt included in their exchanges. She thought for a moment.

"Well, I know that they start meetings with a timed check-in, so everyone shares an update about what they are working on, and then people can respond for a minute or two. Is that what you mean?"

"That's part of it." I needed to be more specific. "Theresa, let's start with your check-in for this meeting. How did people respond to you when you shared?"

She looked confused. So I elaborated. "Were they listening to you?"

"Yes. I guess so."

I continued "How do you know?"

"Well, they were making eye contact with me, and Anna asked some really good questions."

"Good observation, Theresa. So how did you feel after the check-in?"

"I felt good. I felt like I was making progress on the things we talked about, the listening stuff . . ."

She stopped and took a deep breath. "That's why it felt so awful when my idea got shot down." In probing deeper, Theresa revealed that she had been working on and presented one idea in the meeting: a way to streamline the communications between her department and operations management. I asked "Was this communication issue one everyone recognized as an important one?"

"Yes." Then she elaborated somewhat indignantly, "We had solved that issue in my last job, and that's why I suggested the same change in protocol here. And then everyone just shot it down!"

I asked "Did they shoot it down right away?"

She shrugged. "Well, no, not right away."

"What was their initial response?"

Theresa thought hard for a moment. "Well, Laura thanked me."

"Was she sincere about it?"

Theresa looked taken aback. "Yeah. Laura is a pretty straight shooter."

"So the very first reaction you got to your effort was positive? Right?"

Another deep breath. "Right."

"Theresa, this is the kind of information you could choose to listen for going forward." I continued "It's becoming clear that your Hands listening, which is great for coming up with super ideas, needs to take a backseat sometimes at the start of a new initiative, so that you have enough facts and detail, which is your Head listening capability, about how things get done in this workplace. Otherwise, you are going to continue to interpret these encounters through a negative lens. Does that make sense?"

She nodded. But her shoulders sagged. "But it's hard!"

I agreed. "It's not easy, but you have help. You have people on your side. Theresa, is there anyone on your working team you feel you might be able to trust?"

Her first reaction was "No." But then she caught herself. "There I go again!" We both laughed a little. I applauded her realization, and encouraged her to take some time with the question.

She took a deep breath, then she said, "Well, maybe Anna."

"And why Anna?"

"I don't know; she always knows her stuff in the operation meetings, she asks good questions. And she's not one of the ones who needs to talk just to hear themselves talk."

I suggested that she intentionally connect with Anna so that she might have someone onsite who had history with the organization; good boundaries; and a clear, fact-based approach to interpersonal dynamics. Anna was a longtime employee who I knew to be an excellent Head listener. I felt sure that connecting with her would help to widen Theresa's perspective. And it did.

Some months later, in fact, I encountered Theresa at a conference and asked her how she was doing.

She gave me a wide open smile and a big hug. "I'm doing really well!" She had not only retained her job at the same organization but had received word that she was one of three candidates for a supervisory position.

"You've come a very long way, Theresa! So you must be getting along with people a bit better now?"

She rolled her eyes. "Yeah, I can't believe what a bundle of nerves I used to be. Once I stopped convincing myself that everyone had it in for me and focused my listening on what was really happening, my world opened up!"

While Theresa's story illustrates the power of strengthening a Head listening capacity in re-directing a tilt toward negative bias, the Head listening modality can be challenging in a number of other ways, as we'll see in the next chapter.

## The Coach's Perspective: Questions and Applications

1. How would you address Theresa's difficulty in forming good connections with her team?
2. What specific information was she listening for that substantiated her negative impressions?
3. Have you ever tried to get someone to listen differently? Were you successful?
4. How would you suggest that Theresa calm herself emotionally in stressful workplace situations?

## You Might Try This . . . The Fist[5]

Part of my work with Theresa required teaching her ways to calm herself emotionally when she felt on the verge of shutting down or blowing up. There are, of course, a variety of methods that are useful in dismantling an "amygdala hijack". The Positive Intelligence methodology refers to an operating system that is built, over time, by practiced use of mindfulness prompts, known as PQ reps, throughout the day. One of the simplest reps is one that we can do anytime, anywhere. We simply get in touch with our breath, and rub two fingers together such that we can feel the ridges on our fingertips. This way, with consistent practice, when stressful situations arise, the client can realize what's happening in time to do some PQ reps, calm down, and apply a Sage strategy: Empathize, explore the issue further, innovate solutions, navigate towards what is truly important, and then, finally, take action. Effective as these methods are over time, there are some clients who benefit from a more immediate intervention. For Theresa, one of our breakthroughs was a demonstration of "The Fist". This tool, originated by Dan Siegel, is particularly effective if you work with children and teenagers as well.

## Instructions for The Fist

Make a fist. Notice the shape of the fist and the placement of the fingers. Now tuck your thumb under the fingers. It actually looks a little like the human brain.

We can think of the fingers as the prefrontal cortex – the center of mood regulation. The thumb is the amygdala – our fight-or-flight response; some know it as "Lizard" Brain. The job of the prefrontal cortex fingers in this fist is to cover and "calm" the amygdala thumb. Now spread all the fingers out wide. This is what happens when we hear something that makes us "flip our lid", when we have no control over our emotions, when everything goes haywire and we are incapable of listening to any-one other than Lizard Brain (or our Saboteurs in the PQ model). Feel the stress and tension in your hand. If you keep it in this position, it's going to start to hurt. Slowly tuck the thumb back into your palm and gently close the fingers over it. Take a deep breath.

Now your client is likely in a better place to listen to input, messag-ing, and so on that is not feeding negative bias, saboteurs, or Lizard Brain. I also like to remind clients that a regularly formed fist, with the thumb-as-amygdala on top, is what we use when we go to hit someone!

## You Might Try This . . . Breathe to Listen

This exercise comes from the book *The Art of Noticing*[6] by Rob Walker at the School of Visual Arts. I would highly recommend this book as a source for creative inspiration. He quotes a 66-year-old accountant who believes "There is no greater gift than genuinely listening to a person, without interrupting or judging or inserting your opinion." Easier said than done, but his tactic to accomplish this is simple: attentive breathing. Apparently, the accountant was introduced to this skill when he was train-ing to become a sniper in the Marines.

Invite your client, when they next find themselves in an interaction that is triggering, to take a conscious deep breath. You can offer them the chance to practice this within your sessions. The simple act of intentionally taking a deep breath accomplishes three tasks: it slows down the situation, it offers the chance to widen perspective, and it creates an opportunity to listen more deeply and perhaps to feel empathy.

# Notes

1   *Positive Intelligence*, Chamine, Shirzad, 2012
2   *You're Not Listening and Why It Matters*, Murphy, Kate, 2021
3   Assume Positive Intent: https://collaborativeway.com/general/a-ceos-advice-assume-positive-intent/, 2017
4   "The Liking Gap in Groups & Teams", Mastroiannia, A.M., Cooney, G., Boothby, E.J., Reece, A.G., 2021
5   The Fist, Siegel, Dan: www.youtube.com/watch?v=gm9CIJ740xw, 2012
6   *The Art of Noticing*, Walker, Rob, 2019

# A Standardized Patient Story . . . The Limits of Data Saturation

I am lying on a hospital bed. I've just woken up from the anesthesia, and I'm concerned that I can't move my left arm or leg. The nurse told me that the doctor will be in soon to speak with me. She couldn't give me any information about why my movement is restricted, and I'm starting to worry. Then the doctor comes in. He's polite and cordial, and he pulls a chair up to the side of my bed. But he has made no eye contact with me. Now I'm really nervous.

I do work for the Standardized Patient (SP) program[1] at a statewide hospital. The previous paragraph is based on a case I have undertaken often. This type of training is focused on teaching medical students, via comprehensive role play, to incorporate better listening skills and productive interactions within a patient encounter. This program was started in the 1960s but really took off twenty years later to address what had become a national problem within the medical profession; doctors, having graduated from data-saturated programs, had little skill in engaging with actual patients. Over time, health research indicated that the absence of skilled patient communication adversely impacted health outcomes across a broad array of hospital systems. The SP program was launched to address this issue.

At its simplest, SPs take on the role of the patient in a mock medical appointment. They learn the case, symptoms, the patient profile and engage with the medical student as if they were the actual patient with the symptoms in the case. At the end of the session, the SP will give feedback to the student; they rate the emotional impact of the encounter, the level of perceived patient communication skill, and the physical exam proficiency the student exhibits. Examination elements

DOI: 10.4324/9781003296027-9

vary depending on the case, but they begin with a checklist: elements of the exam done correctly, the information that was elicited through adept questioning (that we as SPs were told to reserve unless directly asked), what information was left out, and most importantly, "Did the student exhibit empathy?" A deft touch with empathy – steering between the rocky shoals of caring and invasion – is required. To do this well demands of the student a healthy dose of humility. Empathy, it turns out, is pretty impossible to communicate if the practitioner is convinced of their own expertise.

Leslie Jamison relays a powerful call for humility in an intriguing chapter about her own experiences as an SP in a book titled *The Empathy Exams*.[2] "Humility is a kind of compassion in its own right. Humility means (the residents) ask questions, and questions mean they get answers, and answers mean they get points on the checklist." Points for finding out my mother put me on valium when I was nine years old. Points for getting me to admit my concern that I might have a drinking problem. Points for finding out my father committed suicide when I was seventeen. Points for realizing, as Jamison beautifully puts it "that a root system of loss stretches radial and rhizomatic under the entire territory of a life."

The situation I had relayed earlier of my own SP experience is one of a category of cases titled "Delivering Bad News". This case was built, as most are, on an actual situation. A woman had gone into the ER for pneumonia, but due to a medical error, had woken up unable to move the left side of her body. She had had a stroke on the table as a result of a misplaced IV line. The student is to deliver this news to me, the patient, and be present to the emotional reaction, take responsibility, voice regret, offer information, and suggest next steps. Heart, Head, and Hands: the listening modalities are all lined up in those requirements.

The medical profession, by necessity, is full of problem solvers with deep data retention skills. There is a heavy saturation of Head and Hands listeners. But unless there is also Heart listening, it's difficult for the physician to gain the patient's trust. Part of the mission of the SP program is to empower the patient to see the physician as a partner in their healthcare, not simply as the "expert" who will "fix" the problem. But too much Heart listening can result in loss of authority for the practitioner, as well as mistrust on the part of the patient.

I have to mention that the students I worked with for this session were in their first year of the program. Even so, the wide range of interpersonal skills at work was startling. While many struck a good balance between empathy, responsibility, and authority, others seemed overwhelmed, exhibited huge remorse, and even burst into tears at having to deliver the awful news. The scenario sometimes would come to a halt as no relevant information was given, and little problem solving emerged.

On the opposite end, I saw those (few) who hid behind the corporate "we" as in "We made a mistake and we're sorry". They couldn't bring themselves to take responsibility; they couldn't even look me in the eye. I noticed in myself that, along with my fear, I felt a growing anger in response to this emotional disconnect. These encounters helped me understand viscerally why so much punishing litigation aims directly at doctors and hospital systems.

Within a year or two of being in this program, I learned to pay attention to not only how well the student employs reflective listening and conveys empathy but also what the student may have been actively listening for in these encounters and the role this played in their subsequent diagnostic interpretations.

# Nancy's Story: Jumping to the Conclusive Diagnosis

"Nancy" stares at the computer screen in front of her. Staring back is a middle-aged woman with an expression of slow-motion despair. She confirms her name, Deborah, and her birthdate and then softly reveals what brings her to this encounter: a relentless fatigue, an inability to focus or get anything done, very little joy in the things she used to like to do. She also mentions her forced retirement from a 40-year teaching career due to Covid and her husband with a diagnosis of early onset dementia. Deborah's sadness is so profound that Nancy is momentarily knocked off balance. What can she do to help? She's not a therapist, she's a nurse practitioner! She glances at Deborah's intake sheet, swallows hard and confirms her patient's medication for diabetes, hypertension, and hyperthyroid. Her interest is piqued by the last diagnosis. Finally, a piece of this patient story she can do something about!

Nancy spends the rest of the ten-minute telehealth encounter focused on the hyperthyroid possibility: the amount of Deborah's medication, her last visit with her regular doctor. Has Deborah noted any recent weight loss? Any heart palpitations? Deborah's answers don't really warrant the hyperthyroid focus: She has lost a few pounds, but she's also lost her appetite, and she doesn't experience any increased heartbeats. This frustrates Nancy because she's so sure that the dosage of the hyperthyroid medication is the underlying issue for Deborah's malaise. Hyperthyroidism is an ailment that Nancy is familiar with. Adjusting medication often clears up the problem in a short amount of time. The allotted time for this appointment ends, but very little of it has been spent on Deborah's more difficult diagnosis: depression.

Nancy is a second-year student in a university nurse practitioner program. So far, she has enjoyed the challenges of this focus and has excelled in much of a very intense data-driven curriculum. As part of her second year requirements, Nancy now has classes that involve engaging with Standardized Patients in sessions overseen by faculty. She's gone through a few of these sessions this year and finds them to be, to her surprise, the most challenging aspect of the curriculum so far.

Nancy has bumped up against an important reason for the Standardized Patient program: making clear to a medical student the importance of gaining the trust of the patient so that the patient will reveal the details needed for accurate diagnosis. Instead, many young trainees often want to play to their data-saturated strengths. These students are all efficiency. They rattle through their checklists as if reciting a laundry list of daily to-dos: changes in sleep, appetite, social habits, concentration. They ask leading questions to which the SP can only answer yes or no and often does because they sense their questioner wants to get through this list quickly: "You feel safe at home, right?", "You haven't had any thoughts of harming yourself – right?"

Nancy felt determined to go into medicine after she watched her younger brother lose his battle with cancer. Paul's death and the agony her family went through during his five-year ordeal strengthened her determination to help and support cancer patients and their families. However, her compassionate wish to help has gotten sidelined by the medical profession's emphasis on, and her own aptitude for, data saturation and Head listening.

After her session time runs out, Nancy is asked by Peter, her faculty advisor, "Why did you spend so much time on this one diagnostic focus at the expense of other questions that pertain to possible depression?"

Nancy replied "Well, I wanted to thoroughly flesh out the hyperthyroid prescription issue as so many of the symptoms she presented were in line with problematic dosage".

Peter looked puzzled. "'Many of the symptoms'? Minimal weight loss, fatigue, but . . . what else was Deborah telling you, Nancy?"

"Uhm . . ." Nancy checked her notes.

Peter continued. "Deborah's symptoms and her situation were also very much those of possible major depression, were they not?"

Nancy sighed. "I guess so. But depression is so . . ." She looked away, a little embarrassed.

Peter smiled. "Tricky to treat? Yes. But it's also a major public health problem. It's a constant battle in diagnosis not to run with your first hypothesis, no matter how tempting, because your first responsibility is to the patient – right?"

Nancy nodded.

Confirmation bias, as illustrated in Nancy's story, can be a very pronounced issue in medical diagnoses. Once someone gets attached to seeing a patient's symptoms through a particular lens – all other possibilities, along with any initial curiosity, fade away. This can be dangerous for the patient as well as the practitioner and is thoroughly discussed and dissected in medical residency programs across the country.

# The Coach's Perspective: Questions and Applications

1. As a coach, are you familiar with your own biases? Do you know how you acquired them?
2. In considering your clients, are there foundational biases you suspect might be obstacles to their progress? How have you addressed them in the past?
3. Do any of your clients present as Head listeners? How has this modality proved beneficial for their progress? And how has it hindered their progress?

# You Might Try This . . . Look for Congruence

If you suspect your client may be a Head listener and has exhibited both the abilities and challenges of this modality (there is an assessment in Section 5 of this book to help determine their primary and secondary listening modalities), you might invite your client to get curious and experiment with what they are habitually listening for:

- Next time they listen to learn and gather new information, invite them to become aware of *how* the content is being conveyed: facial expression, body language, and tone of voice, rather than bringing complete attention to the specifics of the content. They might try this when accessing new information from a computer or television:
- Turn down the volume when someone is speaking and see what information can be gathered about this person's frame of mind and experience simply from body language and facial expression. Now bring the volume back up and decide if the face, vocal tone, body, and message are congruent (consistent) or incongruent: are the "how" and the "what" communicating different realities?

# You Might Try This . . . The Filter Exercise

Julian Treasure, in his book *How to be Heard*, offers an excellent exercise in discovering our biases. The Filter Exercise asks us to write about how certain influences have affected our points of view and created the filters through which we process our own experience. This is a powerful exercise no matter the client's listening modality. Encourage your client to write as much as necessary on the following categories to really flesh out how the following influences have shaped their perceptions, beliefs, experiences, and listening. You might encourage clients to write about how these filters and biases developed, along with the benefits and challenges they provide.

Culture Language Values Attitudes Beliefs/Assumptions

Intentions Expectations Emotions Physical Appearance Issues/Expectations

# Head Listening Modality Review: Section Summary

As a reminder, here is a review of the distinct qualities that make up Head listening.

*Head Listeners Listen for:*
- Rational function: Facts, numbers, anything that can be measured
- The known: Established patterns, what's been proven to be true
- Timeframe: The past

*Head Listeners Are Curious About . . .*
- How something works
- Linear progressions
- The factual truth: "What, where, when, and how"

# Strengths and Challenges of Head Listening

*Head listening provides:*
- Balanced, rational, fact-driven listening skills in emotionally charged exchanges
- Well-researched and retained information critical in making decisions and strategizing
- Intentional listening for data and anything already proven and substantiated
- An antidote and challenge to the confirmation biases of others
- The ability to detach emotionally from the situation in order to gain perspective

*Head Listeners are challenged to:*
- Pick up on, value, and retain interpersonal information other than that driven by facts and data
- Stay engaged and centered in emotionally driven conversations
- Own and acknowledge their own conscious and unconscious biases

*Head listener professions and industries (not a complete list):*

| | | | |
|---|---|---|---|
| Data analysis | Engineering | Computer programming | STEM education |
| Science and research | Insurance adjustment | Securities and investments | |
| Cybersecurity | Corporate leadership | Military leadership | Library science |
| Historical research | Aeronautics | Medical research and technology | |

# Positive Intelligence Crossover With Head Listening

I will refer from time to time in this book to the Positive Intelligence model of mindset coaching. I have no agenda to "push" this model on anyone; I offer it only for further exploration. In a nutshell, this model is a method that encourages us to get curious about how we humans get in our own way and what we might be able to do about it via the Positive Intelligence coaching model.

The PQ model has been successfully utilized by companies, corporations, small businesses, and individuals. It provides a consistent framework for greater compassion and mindful practice personally and professionally.

PQ is a system of intentional, proactive change. It starts with the assurance that we don't need to be "fixed" but rather that our mindset gets habitually hijacked by our internal critic (The Judge) and nine different saboteurs. These energies are rooted in some of our best qualities, and they came to our defense during childhood, but as we grow up and out into the world, their influence becomes problematic because they are based in fear. That's why we need to strengthen our five Sage muscles: Empathy, Curiosity, Innovation, Navigation, and Action, in order to reduce the influence of our internal Judge and saboteurs.

# Saboteurs That Align With Head Listening

**Hyper Rational:** Can seem intellectually arrogant, unfeeling. Can be perceived as uncaring in relationships

**Stickler:** Perfectionism, a need for order and organization taken to an extreme

# Sage Powers That Align With Head Listening

**Explore:** The ability to find established truth through thorough research
**Navigate:** Alignment with values, priorities, vision, a wider perspective

# Balance and Amplify

If you feel fairly certain that Head listening is a modality your client struggles to access, invite them to:

- Summarize what they hear out loud at frequent junctures in the conversation (this is highly effective in interviews with medical patients). This will both reinforce detailed information for the listener and give the speaker the sense that what they are saying is valuable enough to repeat back and check for accuracy.
- When listening to someone on, say, a TED talk or a YouTube video, ask your client to stop the recording at certain points and note some of the more granular information they may have heard. Then, once the speaker concludes, you might offer to test their retention.

# Probing Questions for Head Listeners . . .

1. How did you choose your profession?
2. How has it changed you?
3. What keeps you in your occupation?
4. What scares you the most?
5. At the end of your life, what will you look back on that most mattered?
6. What distracts you?
7. How do you keep yourself on task?
8. Who are your heroes?
9. What makes you feel successful?
10. Whom do you trust the most right now?
11. How does it feel to you to be vulnerable?

12. What feels most risky to you right now? How do you feel about that risk?
13. What belief/conviction would you like to let go of?
14. What have you recently discovered or learned that surprised you?
15. What are you most curious about right now?
16. What challenges are you faced with right now?
17. What do you most like to do outside of work?
18. What do you do that lets you lose track of time?
19. What metaphors, if any, are you fond of using?
20. What do you feel is your best contribution to those around you?
21. How do you know when something is true?
22. What frustrates you the most when people communicate with you?
23. What's your preferred form of communication?
24. What helps you learn/retain information the best?
25. Please describe your optimum working environment

# Further Thoughts

Head listeners are excellent at focusing their attention on what is known, proven, and true. They seldom find themselves distracted by random emotional currents and are often seen as leaders in their respective positions. There is often a calm conviction in the way Head listeners convey information that elicits trust in their listeners.

Head listeners also have the potential to dismantle the biases of others, but only if they have a grasp on what triggers and feeds their own. In fact, this modality can be particularly intractable when their specific biases are challenged.

Head listeners can become so embroiled in research that their problem-solving ability becomes reduced, as well as their ability to get along well with others. If they can't see how their own confirmation bias impacts their perceptions, they can become "fixed" in one particular lens, dismissing other points of view and perceptions as irrelevant and untrustworthy. If this attitude is exhibited in a powerful leadership or management role, companies and teams can become much less effective, and innovation suffers.

Strong Head listeners can benefit from the lessons of the next modality: Heart listening.

# Notes

1    Association of Standardized Patient Educators: www.aspeducators.org/
2    *The Empathy Exams*, Jamison, Leslie, 2014

# PART 3

## Listening Styles: Heart Listening – Hearing the Person Behind the Words

# HEART LISTENING MODALITY:

### SECTION SUMMARY

**Heart Listening Provides:**
- Information gleaned from subtle behavioral clues
- Human perspective, empathy, compassion
- Ability to build relationships, partnerships, alliance
- Ability to cultivate and nurture interpersonal trust
- Generous focus & attention to other's needs & priorities

**Heart Listeners Listen for:**
- Emotional Context: Opportunities to build relationship & express empathy
- The Truth Beneath the Words: Vocalics, body language, facial expressions
- Timeframe: The Present — what is happening right now

**Heart Listeners Are Challenged To:**
- Set personal & professional boundaries
- Focus on & trust in information other than emotional
- Identify and own their unconscious biases

**Heart Listeners Are Curious About...**
- How someone really feels
- The emotional context impacting the situation
- Motivations that produce behavior

**Heart Listener Professions & Industries**
(Not a complete list)
- Education • Medicine • Social Work
- Journalism • Psychiatry
- Travel • Non-Profit Leadership
- Childhood Development • Coaching
- Arts and Culture • Humanities
- Gerontology • Counseling

**Benefits & Challenges**

## POSITIVE INTELLIGENCE CROSSOVER

**Heart Listening Provides:**
- Information gleaned from subtle behavioral clues like facial expression, vocal tone, body language
- Human perspective, empathy, compassion
- The ability to build relationships, partnerships, and alliance
- The ability to cultivate and nurture interpersonal trust
- Generous focus and attention to other's needs and priorities

**Saboteurs**
- **Pleaser:** Tries to gain acceptance & affection by helping, rescuing, flattering. Loses sight of own needs, can become resentful & passive aggressive
- **Avoider:** Extreme focus on the positive & pleasant; avoids difficulty, unpleasantness, conflict

**Sage Powers**
- **Empathy:** The compassionate ability to step into another's experience without judgment
- **Navigate:** Alignment with values, priorities, community perspective

# A Playback Story: Listening on Steroids

A woman sits on a stool under strong light. Her interviewer gently asks her questions, while a group of five others, all dressed in black, listens intently to the answers. There are over one hundred people here, but the woman's voice is the only sound in the room. "Sarah" describes uncovering an old secret that has ruptured her family of origin. Before she and her brother were born, unbeknownst to either of them, her mother gave birth to another child, a son. This child was given up for adoption. Only when cleaning out the attic of her parents' home does an adult Sarah discover the evidence: paperwork from the state, depositions, photographs of her mom as an unsmiling young woman, carrying a tiny baby. As she describes how this discovery made her feel, Sarah fights back tears. "Angry." "Devastated." "Betrayed!" And then "Curious". After a few moments and a few more questions, Sarah is invited to sit in a chair positioned at the front of the audience, facing the people dressed in black. The interviewer turns to the group and says simply "I'd like to see Sarah's story told through Perspectives". She then turns to the crowd in the room, and says simply "Let's watch".

This is the initial information that begins a playback sequence. Once the conductor says the words "Let's watch", the players (the five black-clad witnesses) will instantly "play back" the story the teller shared.

Playback Theatre[1] is a story reflection form that has been around since the 70s, with actively practicing companies, prior to the pandemic, in over 60 countries. Drawing from theatre improvisation, music, song and dance, Playback is a deep reflection of a true story shared by a single audience member in real time. The building of an effective playback sequence requires listening skill on the part of the players, the conductor,

DOI: 10.4324/9781003296027-11

and the audience. Because of the intensity of the listening, no one gets to tune out, and with this compelling intimacy, Playback Theatre is one of the most powerful, if relatively unknown, art forms in the world.

Interestingly, it is not unknown in Israel. Israel has 17 companies, many of which are dedicated specifically to create dialogue between hostile factions in the Middle East. How could a reflective story-based art form possibly soften multi-generational animosity in war-torn countries? It's a simple but powerfully effective concept: Once a person is invited to share their story, with authentic emotion in a witnessed forum, and with heartful reflection, the teller feels deeply heard. A degree of anger subsides, and openings are created for productive engagement.

How is Playback relevant to the listening modalities? In order to instantly play back a story, company members have to listen to the teller on multiple levels. Let's start with the conductor.

The conductor's job is complex. Her responsibilities include taking care of everyone's experience: teller, players, and audience. In listening to the teller, her first job is to gain the person's trust. She will employ Heart listening but also tune in to the relevant facts and details for Head listening, along with scanning ahead to troubleshoot the places in the story that might prove difficult to understand for both the audience and the players – Hands listening. She will then name one of 30 improvisational structures that she believes will best amplify the emotional essence of the story. Her listening tasks include all three kinds of listening all at the same time!

I have seen people in the conductor's role who will get a specific vision of the story early on, and then "direct" the teller towards a particular form choice that resonates with that vision. In other words, he actively listens for certain information in the story that will fit with a pre-determined outcome. This can often work brilliantly, but *only* if the emotional essence and message of the story are honored, and I believe this tactic can fail as often as it succeeds, unless the conductor is truly skilled. If the teller feels corralled in any way towards a specific end, he or she can get defensive, muffle themselves into compliance, or simply shut down. If this happens, the experience for everyone will be compromised.

Listening skill needed from the players is slightly different, but still requires attuning to the emotional heart of the story and making sure that relevant facts are utilized in the re-creation.

There is a common pitfall in what the player listens for. If the story has some comedic elements, it can be oh so tempting to decide that the story is funny and to start listening only for events, situations, and relationships that can be utilized for laughs. If I as a player know that comedy is one of my strengths, I might make the mistake of listening only for performance opportunities that will make me look good. Often, this focus can downplay the Heart listening required for an impactful replay and ignores the offerings of others who may have heard the story a bit differently. Additionally, if the conductor chooses a form that isn't necessarily conducive to a comedic playback, I enter the playing arena at a disadvantage. That said, many of the most satisfying playback replays can be greatly enhanced with humor, as long as, again, the heart of the story is amplified as well.

Heart listening can be difficult to sustain over a long period of time. It requires being truly present and available to whatever happens next. This is why Heart listening is a necessary element in any kind of improvisation. My primary job as an improvisor, and as a coach, is to put aside whatever my agenda might be at the start of an interaction and to avoid the temptation to create one as I listen to the teller, my fellow improvisors, or my clients.

I have offered this detailed description of what happens in a particular theatrical improvisation because it is a stark and amplified replication of the listening choices we make in real life – particularly in high-stakes interactions, especially in our coaching sessions.

The key to a successful playback, fruitful interactions in the workplace, in coaching, and in our personal lives is knowing how to tune in to the emotional truth underneath the words without letting that awareness derail our larger intention.

In the Playback example, if a teller speaks softly, fidgets, or avoids eye contact with the conductor, then there are definite messages being conveyed – anxiety, discomfort, fear – regardless of the story being told verbally. It is the conductor's job to address the root of that anxiety to some degree in order to create an effective performing situation for the players, a powerful experience for the audience, and a resonant playback for the teller. The correlation here to effective coaching practice is very strong.

In recent years, applied improvisation has gained a reputation for enhanced communication and business productivity. Chicago's Second

City alum Kelly Leonard explains why in her book: *Yes, And: How Improvisation Reverses "No, But" Thinking and Improves Creativity and Collaboration – Lessons from The Second City*: "The quantitative, strategic, and analytical skills taught in (business) schools do not guarantee success in business, where things tend to be messier and more fluid, and where success often rests on the ability to form winning coalitions that will back a good idea."[2]

Effective Heart listening is vital to building an effective Playback experience, but it's absolutely essential in a coaching interaction. Knowing how to listen, to ask probing questions, to respect a client's experience while gently and intentionally steering them towards self-discovery and more productive behaviors, and to build capacity for resilience in the face of ongoing change – this is Heart listening at its most applicable in coach practice.

With clients in workplace leadership, and for those in management at all levels, applying effective Heart listening skill signals to employees that they are valued as human beings, not just as professionals. Once an employee experiences investment of this kind, they tend to reward their workplace with loyalty and increased productivity. This is reflected in Theresa's story in Chapter 6.

Companies who land on lists of "Best Employers to Work For" have active Heart listening intentionally applied in their company culture. They will often supply benefits like paid leave for employees who are ill or caring for family members, onsite childcare, and flexible schedules. Over the last decades, at least in the United States, these kinds of benefits were offered only in highly profitable corporations. However, with the onset of the Great Resignation post-pandemic, businesses across the board are having to catch on to the economic value of these benefit packages, particularly those businesses that have had issues with employee turnover, especially in fields where workers are in high demand.

*Heart Listeners Listen for:*
- Emotional context
- Opportunities to build relationship and express empathy
- The truth beneath the words
- Vocalics, body language, facial expressions
- Timeframe: The present – what is happening right now

*Heart Listeners Are Curious About . . .*
- How someone really feels
- The emotional context that informs a situation
- The motivations that produce behavior

As you might expect, Heart listening is very much present in teaching, counseling, and medical professions. These skills are utilized in effective journalism and fiction and non-fiction writing, as well as human resource departments in many businesses. It's unfortunate that this kind of listening has been labelled "soft" skills and therefore somehow valued less. The disfunction we witness in business and government often has roots in an absence of Heart listening. It's my belief that the current fractures we suffer from as a culture: red vs. blue, urban vs. rural, black vs. white, wealthy vs. poor, can really only be rectified with the empathy-building qualities of Heart listening. Those who are adept at these skills are truly needed in all walks of life. The intentional development of Heart listening is a worthy endeavor for coaches and clients alike.

# The Coach's Perspective: Questions and Applications

1. How do you utilize your own Heart listening as a coach? Is it a primary strength for you or something you need to intentionally apply?
2. Could your clients make better use of Heart listening? How might you encourage them to practice?
3. What obstacles do your clients encounter that diminishes their Heart listening capacity?

# You Might Try This . . . Listening With Ears, Eyes, and Heart

(From the book *How to be Heard* by Julian Treasure.)[3]
  You can do this with your client. It's also easy to do this via Zoom. Inform your client that this exercise will isolate and then engage, singly, the sensory apparatus involved in listening.

You will sit facing your client and then begin to speak about something or someone important to you – perhaps an experience or how you feel about a loved one.

Your client starts by looking down, attitude neutral, consciously disengaged but listening carefully with the ears. After the first 30 seconds, the client will look up and establish eye contact with you, taking in your facial expressions, body language, tone of voice, and so on. After another 30 seconds, the client is instructed to deepen the connection between you, to feel the feelings and express any non-lingual responses that might come naturally, such as vocal murmuring, facial expressions, nods, posture adjustments, and so on.

Check in with your client as to their experience and share your own. Swap and repeat.

## You Might Try This . . . A Simple Invitation

If you have clients in leadership positions, you may struggle to adjust their perception of time: the amount of time available to them in their cramped schedules or the time left to them in their working lives.

Authentic curiosity, the kind that builds trust, does ask for exploration time. As adults, we often feel we just can't make space for it. As their coach who sees the value of intentional curiosity as a tool your client could benefit from, you might encourage the client to deepen their conversations just a bit with the invitation "Tell me more". "Tell me more about that problem with the supplies", or "Tell me more about why you feel that way about . . . " It's very important that your client ask the question with authentic curiosity, with no attached agenda. This is, of course, easier said than done, but prefacing the invitation with a statement such as "I want to make sure I understand your concerns" could help reduce the temperature of the interaction as well as the pace of the engagement. Curiosity is very much at the center of the next story.

## Notes

1    Playback Theatre: www.playbackcentre.org
2    *Yes, and: How Improvisation Reverses "No, but" Thinking and Improves Creativity and Collaboration – Lessons from the Second City*, Leonard, Kelly, 2015
3    *How to Be Heard,* Treasure, Julian, 2017

# Abbie's Story: The Best Defense Against Anger and Ignorance

Abbie had just moved from a large east coast city to a much smaller New England community. She was renting an apartment in an old house without laundry facilities. Fortunately, there was a laundromat right around the corner, so she found herself doing laundry for a few hours on a Wednesday afternoon. There was no one else in the facility. But that doesn't mean she was alone. After she started a few loads and sat down to read a magazine, she soon realized the futility of that effort. The guy on the radio had been droning on and on since she stepped in the door, but it was only now that she was forced to pay attention to what he was saying.

This was the early nineties. She had heard of Rush Limbaugh but hadn't listened to him. The more he went on, the less she wanted to listen to him now.

The door opened, and a man walked in carrying several large packages. He went behind the counter in the corner and proceeded to stack the packages on the counter, check the cash drawer, and pull out some paperwork. "Ah", Abbie thought. "He either works here, or he owns the place, so I'll just ask him nicely to change the station."

What took place next is why I've chosen to put Abbie's story into this chapter.

Abbie approached the counter and waited while the man finished dealing with his paperwork.

"Excuse me?" she said.

He looked up at her. Blinked twice. "Yeah?"

"Would you mind changing the station?"

"Why." He didn't ask. It was more of a rhetorical question.

DOI: 10.4324/9781003296027-12

"Well." She hesitated. "I'm trying to read, and it's hard with all the talking."

"Really." Again, more of a challenge than a question. "What – You gotta problem with Rush?"

So, at this juncture, I have to ask you, the reader – how would you react to the man's attitude in this situation? I know what I'd do. I'd raise my voice and demand my rights as a customer. I'd point out that I'm the only one here and that maybe, given his choice of audio entertainment – there's a reason he has so few customers . . . *and so on.* Needless to say, that would not end well, and I would have to finish my wash in a sulk, travel next week to the other laundromat across town, or spend big bucks on a washer-dryer.

Abbie didn't do any of that.

Abbie took a deep breath and asked simply, "Why do you like this show so much?" The man seemed taken aback by this question, unsure how to answer, but managed to say "Because the guy tells the truth" – and then "Obviously!" Which Abbie recognized now as an attempt to pick a fight.

"What truth?" she asked calmly.

He was having no more of this.

"You're not from around here, are you?" he said, almost sneering.

"Well, no," she said calmly. "I just moved down the road a few weeks ago."

"Yeah?" he said. "Whaddya do?" Another challenge.

"I am a deejay at a radio station," Abbie said, and she managed a smile.

"Which one?" This time, it was a real question.

"The oldies station". She named the call letters.

"Huh," he said. He was shuffling papers now. No more eye contact. But he continued, "I been thinking I ought to do some radio advertising. Maybe on that station."

"Oh", she said. "Well, I could maybe give you some names of the ad guys and they could set you up."

"Yeah, okay," he said. Then, "That'd be cool. I guess".

There was silence for a minute. Abbie noted that the washer had finished its cycle, and she went to move it into the dryer. As she negotiated her laundry, she noted that the radio had changed . . . to the oldies station.

So what just happened here? What kind of listening did Abbie employ? She had a problem she wanted to solve and decided to take action on it by asking the guy at the desk to change the station. It could have, maybe should have, been a simple exchange, but it got complicated, primarily because of the man's attitude. Abbie sidestepped with the statement about being unable to read with someone talking, which the man recognized as a dodge that he was not going to accept, at which point we could say that Abbie set aside her original intention in favor of . . . what exactly?

In asking a question that went straight to the actual issue, "Why do you like this show so much?" she exhibited sincere curiosity. Which is, unfortunately, so rare in our verbal exchanges that it threw the guy off of his anger trajectory . . . at least temporarily.

Demonstrating sincere curiosity is not as easy as it sounds, particularly when anger is germinating. But Abbie primed herself first in a classically mindful move – she took a deep breath. This allowed her to disengage her own defensive baggage and to create time and space to access her genuine curiosity.

# Curiosity

Curiosity is a absolutely essential tool of Heart listening. Coincidentally, it is also a key element in one of the Sage powers – Explore – in the Positive Intelligence[1] coaching model. As a skill, the Curiosity Quotient[2] has its own designation as CQ and is coming to be considered as prominent as IQ and EQ, particularly in the ability to manage complexity and sparking innovation. In interpersonal engagement, CQ signals respect for, and genuine interest in, the other person's point of view. Curiosity also offers an invitation to engage in intelligent dialogue. The difficulty, particularly in loaded situations, is in keeping one's own anger and defensive instincts out of the exchange. This is crucial in creating trust, which is, of course, the bedrock of any positive relationship, however fleeting or cursory.

Granted, it helped that Abbie worked at a radio station that this man recognized had business value to him. Abbie identified a problem she could help solve (Hands listening) in her offer to connect him with their advertising department. She was able to position herself as an ally not only because she had demonstrated curiosity. When the man again tried to goad her with the "You're not from around here" remark, she displayed some vulnerability in simply telling the man about her relocation, and answering, again non-defensively, the question about where she worked. Despite his disrespectful attitude towards her, Abby demonstrated respect to him by answering his questions openly and honestly. In the end, she didn't even have to repeat her request for a station change.

Not everyone, of course, comes into new situations with this skill intact. In fact, most of us, in dealing with a challenge that pushes our buttons and requires us to employ intentional Heart listening tactics, will resist with everything we can throw at it.

In the Positive Intelligence model – the Explore power is a primary Sage quality. This refers to the ability to slow down and detach ourselves just enough to intercept our automatic response to emotional triggers. Explore power invites us to become curious, to ask questions of others, and most importantly to ask questions of ourselves.

I remember working with a highly competent colleague in a teaching program focused on girls from low-income families. "Sarah" was an expert planner and designed highly engaging curricula, which she bailed on at the first sign of resistance from any of the girls. This left stranded those students who were really working on the planned activities. The focus of the sessions became "therapy" for the girl who was acting out. I would repeatedly flag this as an inappropriate use of our time and not fair to the other girls, and the program was losing momentum because of it, but no matter. Sarah continued to derail our plans in this way. After a few weeks, I came home one evening – got some old china plates out of the basement and began smashing them on the kitchen floor. In this way, I was able to clear out some of the strong emotions that had overtaken me. I realized I was filled with rage to a degree that wasn't appropriate to the program experience. So after I had destroyed dozens of china dishes that I had bought from Goodwill for this purpose, I got curious. What else was going on? Once I asked that question of myself, I suddenly knew.

From an early age, my sister's experience of our family dynamic was very different from my own. Of course, this is not at all unusual between siblings. But in the 70s, no one in my white suburban upbringing was much discussing ADD or hyperactivity disorder. Where Kristine couldn't sit still long enough to focus on much of anything, I could get lost in fascination with books, colors, the conversations around me. I was the "quiet" one and often the "spacey" one. It became clear, as a result of my sister's issues with allergies, hyperactivity and, later, rebellious truancy and so on, that parental attention had turned, fairly exclusively, in my sister's direction. No matter how hard I worked – for grades, for acclaim in editing the school newspaper, for leads in the school plays – nothing seemed enough, at least in my adolescent perception, to garner my fair share.

No wonder I was having issues with Sarah's leadership. I was witnessing the very same dynamic played out between Sarah and the girls in this program. I'm very grateful I was able to release some of that fury (smashing dishes in a safe place is a great way to do that!) long enough to get curious about my reactions. It's a quality I work hard to inspire and nurture in my clients.

As I mentioned in Chapter 2, keeping our innate curiosity alive is difficult for us as adults. There are often acquired beliefs and distractions that prevent us from tapping into this skill. Once we leave adolescence, embark on a professional path, and establish ourselves in adulthood, the pressures of modern life take over, and authentic curiosity gets kicked to the curb. As a coach, one of our assumed superpowers is the curiosity that fuels good questions and helps clients unpack their challenges in unique and insightful ways. One of the benefits to the client of the coaching experience is in designating the time to slow down and invite curiosity and authentic emotional response into the room.

For clients in leadership positions, cultivating curiosity in their team reports and departments is absolutely crucial to innovation and effective problem solving. Unfortunately, in many business settings, curious employees can be considered the source of annoying distractions or even impediments to productivity. An attitude of this kind simply reinforces the status quo: the "business as usual" fallback that can destroy creativity and motivation.

# The Coach's Perspective: Questions and Applications

1. How do you apply your own curiosity as a coach in your practice?
2. Are there clients you work with who could benefit from intentionally applied curiosity in their interactions?

3. What do you think might lay a good foundation for building curiosity as an effective tool?

## You Might Try This . . . A "Curiosity Date"

There's a quote from BF Skinner that I love: "When you run into something interesting, drop everything else and study it."[3] Given the pace of modern life for most of us, this seems like a quaint luxury. I have found, however, that if I can encourage a client to articulate something they would explore *if they had more time*, then it can become possible to find one hour in a busy week to follow a curiosity. This simple suggestion is informed by the "artist dates" in Julia Cameron's *The Artist's Way*.[4]

If you have a client whom you believe could make progress by reclaiming their curiosity, see if you can get them to articulate what they would explore – if they had more time. I've found that most clients, if introduced at the right juncture in our work together, respond well to this prompt. Clients will list anything from equestrian therapy to vegetable gardening to quantum physics. I ask them "What is it that appeals to you about that (activity or subject)?", and their facial expression lets me know that, in their imagination, they are in a place of possibility. Next, I'll ask, "How do you think you might let yourself explore that topic, just for an hour, in this coming week?" Most will mention Googling the subject. Of course. So then I'll say something like "If you were to actually make it a Curiosity Date, on a lunch hour perhaps, where might you go then?" The answers get interesting now: hiking a state park trail, stopping by a garden center, visiting the local university's planetarium. If a client can't really land on anything they are curious about, I ask "When was the last time you visited a bookstore – just to browse?" Browsing at a bookstore for an hour totally counts as a Curiosity Date!

## You Might Try This . . . The Fascinated Anthropologist

I've mentioned the PQ Sage power of Explore previously in this chapter. Sometimes it helps a client to engage more curiosity in their interactions by playing a game. This game, straight from Shirzad Chamine's book *Positive Intelligence*, invites you to become a keen observer of what goes on around you, without – and this is key – trying to change or control what you see. Taking on the role of Fascinated Anthropologist can be very helpful in a difficult situation. The game works to help a client gain a bit of emotional distance to discover things exactly as they are, without bias filters or desired outcomes.

For example, if your client has a conflict with someone, would it be possible for them to let go of their emotional agenda long enough to discover exactly how the other person feels? And why? You might suggest that your client identify two or three discoveries about this problematic interaction and report the results in their next session.

# Notes

1   *Positive Intelligence*, Chamine, Shirzad, 2012
2   "On Passion and Curiosity for Future Success", Friedman, Thomas, https://blog.explo.org/thomas-friedman-passion-and-curiosity-for-future-success, 2013
3   "A Case History in Scientific Method", Skinner, B.F., 1956
4   *The Artist's Way*, Cameron, Julia, 1992

# Richard's Story . . . Empathy Turns the Tables

Richard walks into a quiet hotel lobby in a small northeastern city. It is February. His designer coat isn't quite up to these abysmal winter temperatures, but oh well. Next week, he'll be back in Texas where he belongs. Doing work he is supposed to be doing. If the powers that be will just let him get back to his job. He tries not to get distracted by his upcoming work schedule, or that questionable hire they put on his surgical team. The one he is expected to "make nice" with. "Why are we rewarding incompetence?" He takes a deep breath to shake himself into where he is, right now. Richard is uncertain what to expect from the next few days, and he doesn't like that feeling. So he assumes the experience will probably suck. And he will just have to suck it up. He checks into his room and settles in for the night.

The next morning, early, he showers, shaves, dresses, and attempts to gear himself up for the day ahead. The elevator opens on the eighth floor; he opens the door at the far end of the hall and is greeted by three smiling faces. "Shit." he thinks. "I'm first. Now I have to make small talk with these people. Get me outta here!"

Some years ago, two colleagues and I were hired to do "interventions" with an assortment of highly skilled and very much valued medical practitioners. I had just begun my work with medical students in the Standardized Patient program, so I felt a bit intimidated by working in this way with seasoned practitioners.

The reasons for them attending an intervention came down to this: They may have been "stars" in their respective departments, but they were costing their hospital systems enormously by their inability to work productively with their medical teams. Attrition was particularly high for the

DOI: 10.4324/9781003296027-13

surgical nurses and anesthesiologists assigned to them. Many of these reputable leaders were white, male, and over 55 years of age. They had been shaped in intensely competitive programs and were among those in the highly paid upper echelons of medical expertise and skill. Yet, here they were in "communications training". Their hospital administrators had made it clear to them that they needed to make a good-faith effort here, or their jobs could be at stake. They weren't exactly mandated to come, but they were "strongly encouraged".

The curriculum we used in these trainings included a number of perceptual activities drawn from a variety of sources. We were about to ask our participants to listen from a different head space than what modern American medicine traditionally demands.

After introductions and some warm-up games intended to disarm them, each participant was invited to sit in a chair in the center of the room and share the circumstances that brought him here. The logic behind this first step is so that we can give them the experience of being deeply heard. As facilitators, we may interject with a few questions, but mostly, we simply listen.

Richard volunteered first. "Just to get this over with!" He began with what he does, "Cardiac surgery", and a description of his work environment: "intense", "unrelenting", "never lets up". When asked how he felt about working in this intensity, he first exclaimed "Great! I know what I'm doing and I'm at the top of my game." Then there was silence. An extended silence. We were at a pivot point where Richard could stay on the surface of that statement or take a breath and go deeper . . . and he did. "It's exhausting" he finally admitted. "The pace, the scale, everything's changing all the time, and the pressure . . ." He shook his head. Everyone in the room took a deep breath. Now we were getting somewhere.

I am not going to go into the details of our program, but I will share with you something we ourselves came to know. What surprised us in this training, as we listened to build alliance and partnership, was a sense of what these seasoned professionals were enduring. To a person, each was embroiled in hospital systems undergoing profound change. Each felt that their "hero" status within their departments and practices had amplified expectations beyond what they felt they could manage. Each understood the seriousness of why they were working with us, however resistant they might have been to working in this way.

Half way through the first day, we totally rearranged our agenda to create more space for the participants to share the individual struggles that had brought them here and to create "Activated Scenes" with the stories we heard. As they can prove very useful in working with groups, I will unpack Activated Scenes at the end of this chapter.

As with the Playback scenario that began this section, our intentional Heart listening and the scenes that we designed for these stories created trust not only with facilitators and participants but between the participants themselves. Richard's story inspired others to share more deeply. This was a process that could otherwise have taken weeks, given the amount of armor these gentlemen walked in with. Instead, by Day 2, they were ready and willing to get the most they could out of our work together.

Richard, with as much resistance as he had walking in the door, let down his defenses after we spent that time simply listening to his complicated situation from a place of curiosity and compassion. He ultimately agreed after our training to continue the work we had begun through individual coaching.

The experience of being listened to with full attention and without judgement is so rare for so many of us that, once encountered, it can be transformational. Our need to be deeply listened to in this way is often masked by hostility, resentment, resistance. Once that need is met, however, communication can open to new possibilities.

# The Coach's Perspective: Questions and Applications

1. In general, how do you establish trust in a working relationship?
2. What do you pay attention to? What do you listen for?
3. When working with a guarded client, how have you successfully engaged this person so that your work together can be fruitful?

# You Might Try This . . . The Activated Scene

This tool, outlined in greater detail in Michael Rohd's book *Theatre for Community, Conflict & Dialogue*[1] is primarily useful in group interactions.

I include it here for those purposes. The Activated Scene (AS) may resemble role play or playback or even psychodrama, but it has different structural elements and benefits the group as a whole, in addition to the person who relays the problematic interaction. The primary power for the group is derived from a structured opportunity to deeply listen on multiple levels, to literally step into another's shoes and see the world, as well as the particular situation, through someone else's eyes.

That said, not every group is willing or able to pull together an Activated Scene. For this reason, I have subcontracted with my Playback group as well as other individuals who have experience in improvisation. Groups of clients who have been together for some time may have difficulty letting go of their perceptions of others in the group. This interferes with their ability to "suspend disbelief" when watching their fellow group members take on a role. But if you have even a few members willing to create a small AS, this can serve to inspire others as well.

As the group coach and facilitator, establishing the trust of your group in this process is key. Good Heart listening skills are absolutely crucial in making an AS effective. The group must trust that you care about their thoughts, ideas, and input and that you yourself are open to learning from what happens in the scene.

Additionally, it will be your job to create the AS by asking in-depth questions of your client so that you can create a story, and flesh it out, using the following checklist.

# Elements of an Activated Scene

- A believable, realistic situation
- A previously structured, but not scripted, scene – ideally crafted by the facilitator and based on a client's experience
- The scene is primarily built around a moment of decision – What will the client choose to do?
- There are clear relationships, intentions, circumstances, location, activity, high stakes, and very active and intentional listening.
- The conflict is clear
- The client is the protagonist
- A clear antagonist

- Clarity about what the client wants and does not want
- The client's failure to get what they want
- The reason for failure clearly being the strong actions, choices, and attitudes of the antagonist
- Clarity that the client had internal forces and desires that contribute to an inability to succeed

It's important for you as the coach/facilitator not to structure the scene towards a conclusion that you consider the "right" one. In order for the AS to resonate with the client and the rest of the group, it has to be as true to the original experience as possible.

At different junctures in the AS, you will be required to stop the action where a decision is to be made. You can then ask the group the following questions:

Was this scene realistic? (If not, ask specifically how it can be improved – and do the AS over again. This repeat goes a long way towards establishing trust in the process.)

- What was happening? What was going on?
- Who is the main character, and what do they want? What did they learn?
- How did they go about getting what they wanted?
- What prevented them from getting what they wanted?
- What else could they have done to get what they wanted? What other choices did they have?

These questions ideally will garner more than one answer. At the point of suggestions for choices, you could ask the person who came up with that option to replace the protagonist in the group in order to demonstrate how that alternative could work. Or, you could simply suggest that the original protagonist choose from the suggested options and see if one of those might be better. It is very important to gather as many options as possible. This not only expands the list of alternatives for the client whose story has just been witnessed, it also engenders the creativity of the group as a whole.

Additionally, it is very important that you minimize the possibility of debate and argument within the group. This can be accomplished by making sure that each comment is directed to you and you alone. Your job is to listen deeply to suggestions and reactions, to ask further questions where needed, and to validate the contributions that come forward.

## Challenges in Facilitation

The most important question in the process is the first one: Is this realistic? This applies not only to the original situation but to the alternative suggestions as well. It also applies to the portrayal of the protagonist and antagonist. The original "cast", as well as their replacements, have a responsibility to match the high stakes, emotion, and behaviors of the original problem. This is not easy, particularly after the scene has already played out a few times. And yet, the integrity of the depiction, for the group as well as for the client, is very important.

Let's see how this could play out with a brief example drawn from Richard's experience. He relayed a problematic dynamic between himself and the chief administrator in his hospital system. I would ask for details of the situation, including emotional responses during and after the interaction. I would then ask Richard to choose someone to play him in the scene. I would choose his antagonist. In a sense, I am empowering Richard to co-design his own AS. This investment can transform a participant from reluctant to engaged.

I will then outline the events in the scene – writing them on a white board or other means of display and check back with Richard to make sure I've left nothing out. Then the AS proceeds. The two parties relay the scene in its entirety. I ask Richard and the rest of the group whether the depiction is realistic. If not, I direct the players to make adjustments based on viewer input until the group is satisfied. Then I'll direct the AS to begin again, and they will take it to the point of decision. I'll then stop the action and ask the first set of questions, gather suggestions, and, if warranted, get substitutes for the protagonist. I'll also assign someone to list the suggestions for alternative actions, decisions, and behaviors.

Ending the scene on a positive note is not the goal. That may be surprising to some. The point of this exercise is to give everyone an experience built on deep listening, empathy, and the discovery of alternative actions in challenging situations. The benefits are many: The client feels deeply heard by you and the group as a whole, the group has an opportunity to help a fellow client sort through problematic situations, and the truism of "No right answers but many good possibilities" is reinforced in a strongly experiential framework.

Trust requires an investment of time, focus, and energy. Building trust starts from a willingness to be authentic and a grounding in competent experience but also in a genuine desire to listen with empathy and without attempting to change what you hear.

What we managed to do in the situation outlined here is gain the trust of these medical practitioners not by impressing them with any expertise on our part but from deeply listening to their situation from the beginning of their work with us. Once they had experienced the relief that being seen and heard offers, they could trust that there would be value in what we were about to offer them.

The next chapter offers an opportunity to dig into listening to gain trust as a life-or-death skill. Literally.

# Note

1    *Theatre for Community, Conflict & Dialogue*, Rohd, Michael, 1998

# Building Trust When the Stakes Are High

My father was a decorated Marine. He was too young and skinny to fight the Nazis in WWII, but by the time the Korean "conflict" blew up, he was trained, fit, focused, and ready. He rose to the rank of second lieutenant, in charge of a platoon in the brutal Korean winter.

Like so many men of his generation, he did not speak much about his time in battle, but he did say this: "I learned the importance of listening with more than my ears, and that kept me alive". He became adept at interviewing prisoners not because he understood the language (he had an interpreter for this) but because he could read facial expression, gestures, and body language well enough to accurately discern truth from lies about the enemy's position, their resources, their plans.

Our world doesn't focus much on listening as a critical skill in hostile and dangerous situations. Consciously or unconsciously, we turn to guns, knives, and pepper spray to make us feel safe. I've decided to include a section here on listening as a life-preserving act so that you, in coaching your clients to increase their listening effectiveness, can impress upon them the importance of listening to build trust and reduce danger in their own interactions. If we could rely on our ears more than our weapons in hostile situations, or those that we perceive to be, our world would be profoundly changed.

Many coaches who work with victims of abuse will recognize the hyper-awareness required to survive such situations. Some clients can instinctively read the temperature in a room such that they can divert attention; change the subject; or, if possible, and it isn't always, find a way to simply remove themselves from loaded and problematic interactions. Over time, these people have honed listening skills to such a degree that they depend on them for their very survival.

DOI: 10.4324/9781003296027-14

In the Positive Intelligence (PQ) model, one of the nine saboteurs is the Hyper-vigilant.[1] Those afflicted with this coping strategy are always attuned to their environment, hyper-aware of shifts in vocal tone and group dynamic, seldom able to let down their guard and trust that they are safe in their own skin. This is an exhausting way to live. However, those who have suffered abuse in a variety of situations for an extended period of time have, by necessity, developed hyper-vigilance as a coping strategy. This is also true for many forms of PTSD.[2]

One of the facets of the PQ model I have come to appreciate is that each of the saboteurs has, at its foundation, positive qualities. For hyper-vigilance, a key quality is a strong sense of contextual awareness, of which Heart listening is foundational. As it turns out, there are actual professions that have evolved to the point where this listening modality is an absolute requirement. One of those areas is conflict negotiation. Another is the CIA.

A note here before we dive in. I offer this chapter as an exploration. I have no experience in negotiating with anyone about to commit suicide, nor can I claim to be an undercover CIA operative. I've worked with no clients in either field. But I am curious to explore just how far Heart listening can extend as a critical skill into fields with very high stakes, with life-or-death consequences.

Amaryllis Fox writes about her experiences as a CIA agent in *Life Undercover – Coming of Age in the CIA*.[3] It's a fascinating and suspenseful story, of course, given the topic, but I reference it here because Heart listening is an underappreciated yet vital skill in working undercover.

"At their best", Fox writes, "Agency officers are charged with a different kind of defense: the act of listening, learning, building relationships, cultivating trust." She calls this "soulful work, investing in a relationship with the adversary."[4]

While desperately trying to stop Al Qaeda from obtaining the uranium necessary to create "dirty bombs", Fox shares the story of meeting her intel source, Karim, for the first time in Iraq.

"'What brings you to Erbil?' I ask him, the opening of oral bona fides, an exchange of predesignated sentences to confirm each other's identities.[5]

'The call of the mufti,' he replies. Most assets recite their bona fides with boredom or irritation, but he says the words with exquisite feeling as though they were not only true but urgent."

Notice here what Fox observes in Karim's response, giving her rich information about his emotional state of mind.

Karim reveals that his Chechen contact has "gone dark" and that a vital intel source on Al Qaeda is in jeopardy. He now needs a new source, one that the United States can hopefully provide. This is a very tense meeting. Karim suspects he is being watched.

"How long do you have?" Fox asks.

"'Five minutes' he repeats, holding my eye. I search his gaze for a beat. He looks frightened inside there, somewhere under the calm demeanor."

She shares the possibility of a new connection, Jakab, to replace the lost Chechen source.

"'He's credible?' Karim asks. In his voice I hear the subtext: Can I bet my life on using his name?'"

She provides Jakab's information to Karim.

"He takes it from me, his eyes still on mine. They are impossibly sorrowful, like a Miyazaki character's searching for someone to trust."

She assures him "We'll find a way through this.' He nods, as though he doesn't quite have the confidence to speak without crying.

'You're doing the right thing Karim.'"

Notice all the observation going on here; the listening off the surface, the attunement to subtle cues in vocal tone, shifts in vocal tension, facial expression. Fox is highly adept at reading the truth beneath the words. She has to be, and so does Karim, for personal safety and for success in a mission impacting entire countries. Trust in high-stakes interactions like these can only truly be built through subtle revelations of vulnerability and the Heart listening required to read them.

The superpower of Heart listening is, of course, empathy. The ability to extend, as well as elicit, empathy is key in the situations Fox shares in her CIA experience. Now, we are about to look at how empathic Heart listening can literally save a life through the skills required in effective high stakes negotiation.

Mark Goulston, in his book *Just Listen*,[6] begins with this story: "Frank is sitting in his car in a large mall parking lot, and nobody is coming near him because he's holding a shotgun to his throat". Frank is in his 30s, suddenly unemployed, homeless, and alone, as his wife and children have just left him. The situation has spiraled down to this point – a shotgun at his throat and a SWAT team at his back. It's been this way now for a few hours. The negotiator first on the scene has gotten nowhere with his pleas to Frank to embrace "another way out."

Enter Detective Kramer, trained in the deep and empathic listening espoused by Goulston and at the heart of Heart listening. "'I'll bet you feel that nobody knows what it's like to have tried everything else and be stuck with this as your only way out, isn't that true?"[7] Notice the empathy in that statement, as if the speaker were verbally sitting right beside Frank and looking at life through his frantic and red-rimmed eyes.

After he gets over his initial shock that someone may possibly understand his point of view, he responds. "Yeah, You're right! Nobody knows, and nobody gives a f*ck!" This is progress.

Kramer continues "And because nobody knows how bad it is and nobody cares and because nothing goes right and everything goes wrong, that's why you're in your car with a gun wanting to end it all. True?"

For the first time, there is a hint of calm in Frank's response. "True".

Then comes the invitation from the detective. "Tell me more." And Frank complies, he lists off all his agonies. Frank is then asked to be specific about his feelings: "All this has caused you to feel . . ." angry, helpless, hopeless, frustrated, overwhelmed . . . ? Frank quietly responds "Fed up."

What has happened here? Frank has experienced, for once, and in too long a time, what it's like to be listened to, empathized with, deeply heard. He's been asked to step outside his experience long enough to name his emotions. This provides a small pause in his mental anguish long enough to access what Positive Intelligence considers the Sage mindset. Those trained as stage actors may see in this pause a way of building a "second attention" – being able to be present to the emotions in the story they are telling, as well as the real-time reactions of the audience. Coaches and therapists familiar with the EMDR model of trauma therapy[8] might recognize this as dual attention. Once this happens, Frank can calm down enough to consider possibilities other than violence. But before he could get to that place, he had to experience being deeply heard; he had to experience Heart listening.

Most of our clients, hopefully, will not find themselves in circumstances that produce Frank's level of pain and desperation. Regardless, Heart listening is something we all use as a way to extend our "radar" in unfamiliar situations, such as a new job, as in Theresa's story, or in meeting a significant other's family for the first time, as with a client I will call Brandi.

# Notes

1   *Positive Intelligence: Hyper Vigilant*: https://support.positiveintelligence.com/article/113-hyper-vigilent

2   *Symptoms and Diagnosis of PTSD:* www.verywellmind.com/requirements-for-ptsd-diagnosis-2797637

3   *Life Undercover: Coming of Age in the CIA*, Fox, Amaryllis, 2020

4   *Life Undercover*, Fox, page 91

5   *Life Undercover*, Fox, page 111

6   *Just Listen*, Goulston, Mark, 2015

7   *Just Listen*, Goulston, pages 5–6

8   EMDR Therapy Model: https://emdria.org/about-emdr-therapy/

# Brandi's Story: Listening to Survive – and Decide

Very early on in my practice, I did work with Brandi as she weighed whether to marry the man she had been living with for a year or so. She had just come back from an extended visit with his family. I've included her experience here as an example of listening to find one's way through a new and difficult situation.

"Brandi" and "Shawn", residents of Manhattan, were visiting his parents in the upper midwest for an extended period of time. Brandi had spent a few evenings with "Mitch" and "Deb" and could sense some tension in their relationship, but she felt she got along with them pretty well individually. The 14 days she spent in their home, however, proved to be powerfully educational.

Brandi was a petite and energetic young woman in her mid-20s. Stylishly dressed, she had a lovely smile that seemed to explode across her face at odd junctures in our conversation.

At our first meeting, I asked Brandi to describe what inspired her to connect with me. She shifted in her seat before answering; her wide gray eyes drew an arc over my head from left to right.

"Well, I need to make a decision, and I am wrestling with it."

That much was clear. I affirmed her seeking support for working through this decision and waited for more details.

"Shawn and I have been living together for a little over a year, I guess?" Another shift in her chair. "But last month we went to stay with his parents for a couple weeks and it was the first time we had really spent time with them since Shawn and I met? And . . . it was . . . weird." She looked down at the floor and paused.

DOI: 10.4324/9781003296027-15

"Tell me more about that." I suggested. "Weird how?"

She cleared her throat, gave me a dazzling quick and fleeting smile. "Well, it was fun during the day. We took his brother's boat, a pontoon boat, out on the lake and fished and swam and things? It was fun."

"But then . . ." She paused, took a deep breath, and directed the rest of her story to the ceiling.

"Every time we got back to the house to have supper, everyone would start drinking. They'd pop open beers around 5 when his mom – Deb – would put supper together. I offered to help and that was kind of okay, you know. I get along okay with her I guess. But then . . ." Brandi took a deep breath. "Well, after everyone had a few beers. . . . I had one, you know, just to be social, but I'm not a big beer drinker." Another deep breath.

"We would all sit down to dinner and then it would start." Another deep breath. I watched her purse her lips and look at the floor.

I pressed her gently. "Can you tell me more, Brandi? What would start?"

The rest of the story was directed at the floor.

"Well, first Mitch – Shawn's dad – would say something about the food. Like, if we had chicken or something, he'd say 'Oops, this piece didn't get cooked.' And then Deb would say 'Well, Mitch, maybe you could try cooking dinner sometime, not that we'd survive that experience.' And it would go downhill from there."

"Downhill?" I asked.

"Yeah, you know, they'd pop open more beers and start bringing up old shit to fight about, and then everybody else would put in their two cents and it would just get louder and louder." "It was really . . . weird."

"This would happen how often?"

"Every night."

I took that in. "And you were there how long?"

"Two weeks."

"I see." My turn to take a big breath. "Brandi, how did all of this arguing make you feel?"

She paused. "It confused me. I didn't understand what was going on. And it would happen every time we ate dinner."

"I hear that this confused you." The expression on her face was very sad. "Were you feeling anything else?" I asked this question with as much neutral curiosity as I could.

"Uhmm." Another arc over me with the eyes. "I felt kind of . . . scared, I guess".

"Very understandable." I paused before asking the next question. "Where was Shawn in all of this?"

Brandi sat up straight and became very still. "Well, he's never really gotten along that well with his mom, so . . . he got into all the arguing too."

"Did he talk to you about it afterward?"

A small shake of her head. "No".

"Did anyone say anything about the arguing at all?"

Another quick and fleeting smile. "Nope. It was like it was just . . . normal behavior for them."

A question suddenly popped into my head, so I asked, "Brandi, you said this went on every night for the two weeks you visited them, right?" She nodded. "And that you felt confused and scared?"

"Yes."

"So, how did you cope with this situation – these dinners where everyone is getting more and more hammered and angry?"

She seemed taken aback by the question. "Uhmm. Well . . ." Her eyes travelled around the room and then settled on me, and she looked suddenly very unsure. "You're going to think I'm weird."

"Try me." I said. "You have described a very weird situation. One that happened on a nightly basis. I'm really curious how you dealt with it."

Another deep breath.

"Okay. After a couple of nights of this, I started counting the sounds of the beer cans being opened, the 'pops', you know? There was kind of a pattern to it. By the time the tenth can was opened, everybody's voice would get louder and they'd start interrupting each other. So that became my signal." She stopped.

"Go on." I prompted.

"Okay. I started to find places I could go to get away from the dinner table when they'd all start in."

"Places?" I asked. "Where were these places?"

Brandi laughed a little. "Well." She looked embarrassed. "They had this really nice garden in the back yard? So . . . after awhile I would take my plate and sit out in the garden with the flowers and the tomatoes." She shrugged. "Weird, right?"

"Not at all. Brandi, it sounds to me like you felt trapped in a hostile environment that made you feel unsafe, and you found a coping strategy."

She looked relieved. "Thanks. I guess."

"But what did you do when it rained?"

"Oh right. Well . . . one time there was a big thunderstorm around suppertime. The thunder started up around, I don't know, 4:30, and I thought 'Well, no garden tonight!' So I decided to take a plate up to the room we were staying in." She continued. "There was a TV in there? So I would eat dinner and watch the news with the sound way up."

"The sound way up?" I asked.

"Yeah, to drown out the arguing."

My turn to take a deep breath. My heart was breaking for this young woman in front of me.

"Wow." I said. At that moment it was pretty much all I could say.

She took a deep breath and looked at the floor. "Yeah."

"Brandi, you said at the beginning of our conversation that you had a decision to make. Can you tell me what that's about?"

A shadow fell across her face. "He wants us to get married."

Before I conclude Brandi's story, let's look at the coping strategies she employed in this situation. While we can believe that a family with consistent dinnertime vitriol does not necessarily present a clear danger, it does create a context filled with the kind of unpredictability that can quickly turn violent, given the right toxic brew of elements.

What strikes me now as I recall this story is the way Brandi employed listening to cope as best she could and to cue her safety strategies. While she was not necessarily a hostage, she nonetheless experienced the feeling of being trapped where she was, in a family dynamic over which she felt she had no control. In response, she began to use her ability to listen beneath the surface of noise and argument to tune in to environmental cues. She listened for the tenth beer can pop top, she listened for the rise in voices and the increased interruptions. The thunder outside let her know that she needed a plan B to get through yet another angry and clamorous family dinner.

It can be tempting, in hindsight, to judge someone who stays in a traumatic situation. I can look at this with the experience of many years, and want Brandi to more strongly stand up for herself and somehow "teach" these people a lesson, or just pack her bags, call an Uber, and get the hell out. Though she attempted to minimize how frightened she was, Brandi clearly experienced this encounter as traumatizing. Yet she stayed. Why?

I've been offered a piece of wisdom recently "Fear, when flipped, is about Desire". Brandi clearly wanted this relationship with Shawn to work. It was one in which she had invested time and significant emotional connection. She described many of Shawn's positive qualities: tenderness, honesty, humor, resilience, as desirable in a mate, yet this venture into Shawn's original family dynamic, and the role he played in it, stopped her in her tracks when the possibility of marriage arose.

After another few sessions in which Brandi was able to further process some of her emotional stress, I suggested she and Shawn seek couples therapy prior to making any decisions. When I checked in with her a few months later, she revealed that Shawn had resisted and finally refused to enter into any kind of therapy, so she had left him. Brandi cried on the phone as she revealed this information. I acknowledged the difficulty of the decision but also applauded her taking needed time with it and ultimately choosing to honor her own internal truth.

## The Coach's Perspective: Questions and Applications

1. What does the phrase "Fear, when flipped, is Desire" bring up in you?
2. If Brandi and Shawn had sought counseling with you, what would you want to tune in to in terms of the way they listen to each other?
3. What did the descriptions of Brandi's comportment and behavior tell you about her situation?

## You Might Try This . . . 3–2–1 Observation Practice

This exercise is highly effective for building calm concentration and focus. It is also excellent in helping encourage building semi-detached awareness in emotional interactions.

The next time you have a session with a client who is particularly anxious or distracted, have them take a few deep breaths. Then invite them to focus on three things in their surroundings that they can see. Encourage them to limit their focus to those three things for 20–30 seconds or so. Then ask them to close their eyes and focus on three things they can hear. Ask them to try to tune in to subtle sounds where they are – to discover sounds they may not have heard before. Again, encourage focus on these three things. The same sequence applies to three bodily sensations. Then ask them to take a deep breath and open their eyes. Now ask them to limit their attention to two things they can see (these can be two of the same things seen before or different items). Repeat with two sounds heard and two sensations felt. Finally ask them to keep their eyes open and focus on one thing seen, one sound heard, and one sensation felt. After a few deep breaths, ask them to note any differences they may be aware of in their mental state now, as compared to how they felt when they began the session. Most clients report a marked reduction in anxiety, stress, and distraction.

# Confirmation Bias and Heart Listening: A Recycle Story

Because so much of the listening focus in this modality has to do with tuning in to emotions, adept Heart listeners need to be particularly alert and aware of their own confirmation biases. As I've noted before, this bias encourages us to tune in to and reinforce what we already believe rather than expanding our own learning to embrace new information that may conflict with those beliefs. A strong confirmation bias functions as reinforcement for what we want to believe about ourselves, as well as the world around us. In particular, it is a highly effective filter that allows us to tune out and sometimes literally not even hear new information, contrary opinions, or proven facts if they conflict with what we already "know". This next story serves as an example of one of my own confirmation biases and will illustrate this point.

## A Recycle Story

Since my early teens, I have strongly resonated with the ideas behind "Renew, Recycle and Re-use". I shop at thrift stores, I do my best to fix things, and I've been a consistent and committed recycler for decades. So the disturbing news that China was no longer taking the majority of our recyclables was a reality I didn't know how to process. So I didn't. I did what many of us continue to do – just sort the stuff the way we always have. The other night, my 20-something daughter put a plastic yogurt cup in the trash, and when I corrected her, she came back at me with "Mom! China isn't taking our plastics anymore. Get over it! All we can recycle now is paper, glass, and cardboard." Right.

DOI: 10.4324/9781003296027-16

I have a few choices here. I can continue to ignore the facts, give in to my confirmation bias, and do what I've always done. And our town is more than happy to continue this illusion while quietly trucking our plastics off to the landfill. But my confirmation bias feeds my emotional need to feel like a good person helping to take care of our planet. My heart listening on this subject is tuned only to the reinforcement of this self-concept. If that need is strong enough, and I'm truly committed to recycling, I can put my Head listening skills to use and look clearly and objectively at the cold hard facts of recycling in my state and my county. I can then, but really only then, put my problem-solving Hands listening to work in seeking out solutions built on a new reality based on facts.

Within this story is another danger inherent in confirmation bias – it can present a significant obstacle to critical thinking. It allows me to be lazy in my commitment to recycling, as it affords me a comfortable emotional bubble built on selective perception and wishful thinking. As the inverse of the truism "Seeing is believing", confirmation bias functions instead according to "Believing is seeing", and for our purposes, "Believing is hearing".

The more we dig into biases, the trickier our mental terrain becomes. Loran Nordgren and David Schonthal are university professors focused on the "friction" that obstructs new ideas and positive change. Their best-selling book *The Human Element: Overcoming the Resistance That Awaits New Ideas*[1] invites an even closer look into biases. The audience for the book is largely entrepreneurs and sales professionals, but their concepts are quite intriguing when applied to listening and problematic behaviors.

The human mind, as coaches know, is highly resistant to change. For psychologists, this tendency is known as *status quo bias*. Marketers know it as the *familiarity effect*, or *inertia*. The model Nordgren and Schonthal provide to unpack the status quo bias is composed of four elements:[2]

1. **Inertia** – The powerful need to stick to what we know, no matter the negativity it produces or the problems it intensifies. Theresa's initial reluctance to undertake coaching had much to do with inertia.
2. **Effort** – The real or erroneously perceived effort we expect to have to undertake in order to make change. Gretchen was, at first, experiencing a feeling of overwhelm at the thought of improving her

presentation skills. She had amplified in her mind how much time and effort would be involved in the process.

3. **Emotion** – Often business clients come into coaching weighted with fears of the "unintended consequences" of making needed change. We can see this concern arise in clients who are tackling substance abuse once they consider the impact of change on their friends and social supports.

4. **Reactance** – The active and often hostile reaction to change that is demanded from outside authorities. For clients like Richard, who have been "strongly encouraged" by their managers to make needed change, reactance can take the form of mental armor that requires much patience, empathy, and Heart listening on the part of a coach in order to dismantle.

Confirmation bias doesn't just apply to information in the world around us; it has potential to impact our relationship with ourselves, as well as our beliefs about what we are capable of, as illustrated in the next chapter.

## The Coach's Perspective: Questions and Applications

1. What do you consider your own biases? How do they affect your work with clients?
2. Do some of your clients hold biases that are obstacles to their progress? Have they been able to make progress once they become aware of them?
3. Are there particular biases that are foundational to many clients in your particular coaching niche? If so, what are they?

## You Might Try This . . . Testing for Implicit Bias

If this section sparks curiosity in you or your clients about which confirmation biases may be operating underneath problematic behaviors, I encourage you to take a short but highly effective test – the Harvard

Implicit Bias test[3] – to find out. I was pretty surprised to discover I had quite a few biases formed from traditional gender expectations. Becoming conscious of these has increased awareness for me in many associated areas.

# Notes

1    *The Human Element: Overcoming the Resistance That Awaits New Ideas*, Nordgren, Loran, and Schonthal, David, 2021
2    *The Human Element*, and Schonthal, page 6
3    The Harvard Implicit Bias Test: https://resources.lmu.edu/dei/initiativespro grams/implicitbiasinitiative/whatisimplicitbias/testyourimplicitbias-impli citassociationtestiat/

# Maya's Story: Challenging Limiting Self Perceptions

Maya loved her job as a residence social worker at Harper Community. She is an empathic listener, and appeared, for a long time, to have an inexhaustible supply of patience with a troubled clientele. But the state funding that supported her position fell to the last round of budget cuts, and now Maya needs to look for another job. Although she would never admit it, she was getting burnt out in her position with Harper, and the news of her layoff came with just a little bit of relief. She's at a critical juncture in her professional life; she knows she can get another social work position, perhaps with a larger, more fortified institution. Or . . . she could begin searching for something completely different.

Maya would qualify as a primary modality Heart listener. She has a reputation for making friends with anyone, and people trust her from their first encounter. But she has begun to experience a significant downside of applying her Heart listening skill so prominently in her career path – namely the struggles Heart listeners often have in setting boundaries and prioritizing their own needs. For the last seven years, Maya has so completely poured herself into her position with Harper Community that she has little focus, time, or attention for much else. She doesn't date, she has no children or even a pet, and she continually struggles financially. She has managed, however, to maintain strong friendships, what social scientists term "social capital",[1] which will prove to be a valuable resource. Because she builds rapport quickly and is possessed of a steady countenance and an empathic quality that builds trust, her friend Denise believes that Maya just might be a terrific sales person in the company she herself works for – ScholasticSource Servicing, Inc.

DOI: 10.4324/9781003296027-17

Maya has never imagined herself a sales person – let alone someone who can grasp the intricacies of the multiple software applications used in colleges across the globe. When Denise suggests it over lunch, Maya thinks she's joking.

"Oh c'mon girl. I could never wrap my head around all that tech stuff, let alone sell other people on it!"

But Denise is ready for this pushback.

"You've been working on other people's problems for a long time. You've built a skillset that you probably think only applies to social work. But Maya, you use computer systems every day to keep track of clients – right? It's the same principle used in tracking sales prospects. And remember last year, when Harper completely re-did their entire IT platform? You were the one who taught some of the others how to use the new software – right?"

"Well, I guess so." Maya admitted. "But it took me a long time to grasp it myself."

"The point is, you did grasp it, enough to teach others." Denise continued, "And as your friend, I need to encourage you to use those same teaching skills and develop a few more so that you can take better care of your own life for a change!"

Maya was surprised by her friend's forthright assessment of her skills, along with the tiny flame of excitement that just ignited inside her. But Denise's challenge also made her gulp. Could she really learn a whole new skillset that would apply to sales? She might have to reassess her outdated, "used-car-salesman" assumptions about salespeople. She might have to start redefining the way she thinks of herself, and she will need to begin learning to listen in a whole new way.

Have you ever found yourself in Maya's position? I know I have – on multiple occasions. It's scary and uncomfortable. Clients in white-collar professions often take their job titles for granted. But when a position is suddenly snatched out from under them, their world tilts sideways and does a face plant on the floor. Additionally, the occupations that sustain clients, particularly positions they have had for a long time, often utilize a limited number of skillsets and require specific listening styles over others. Maya can rely on her ability to connect with people quickly and easily, as well as her capacity to listen deeply and make clients feel heard. But she will also need to begin using more of her Head listening to grasp and retain information critical to a new position. Can she do it? Will she even want to?

In a world churning with change, it's difficult to embark on any new venture that puts us at risk, especially when it comes to our own self-perceptions and professional definitions. Denise has articulated a challenging proposition for Maya – to change her self concept into one where she is not only an empathic and trusted listener but someone who can learn, grasp, and retain established information and then convince prospective clients to sign on to it. This transformation starts within Maya, not outside of her.

When Maya came to me for help, she was trying to discern her next steps.

"I know I need to find something soon. But I don't want to make the wrong choice!" The struggle of weighing where to put her focus and energy now was written all over her lovely face.

My first questions tend to be contextual. "Maya, when you say you 'need to find something soon', what or who is telling you this?"

She looks at me incredulously. "Well, fear of going broke, obviously!"

I probe a bit deeper. "Are you currently on the verge of going broke?"

Maya thinks for a moment. "Well, I can access unemployment if I have to. I did get a small severance, so that will tide me over for a bit. But I don't want to lose health insurance, so I'd rather find something sooner rather than later."

Yes. Health insurance benefits and the fear of losing them weigh heavily in the employment decisions of so many Americans of working age.

"So Maya, please don't answer this question unless you are comfortable doing so. Are you struggling with an illness or a chronic condition of some kind right now?"

"No. I'm pretty healthy."

"I'm glad to hear it." I hesitated. "The reason I'm asking. . . . Job loss is, as you are experiencing, one of the most impactful stressors people have to endure. And the temptation is to 'fix' the problem as quickly as possible. I know this from my own experience, Maya. And it often results in unhappy choices and wasted time."

Maya nodded and folded her hands in her lap. When she did this, I suddenly felt a very odd sensation – as if I were a teacher correcting the behavior of a small child.

Maya's Listening Style assessment put her firmly in the category of primary Heart listener. And her Positive Intelligence assessment[2] high-lighted The Please[3] as her strongest saboteur. I was seeing this played out in front of me in Maya's suddenly submissive posture.

My work with Maya was to encourage her to give herself permission to take the time she needed to put her Heart listening skills to use *to serve herself*. Our work together was increasingly focused on mindful-ness techniques to slow down the voices of panic in her head so that she could uncover and tune in to her own internal promptings toward a new professional focus. In addition, we would work to strengthen the Positive Intelligence framework of the five Sage qualities: Empathy, Explore, Innovate, Navigate, and Action[4] This was the general strategy that guided our work over the next three months.

Then one day Maya came into our session looking as if she were unu-sually distracted. She said she was feeling very nervous, but I could tell there was something else brimming up from under the tension. She had just had her discussion with Denise, and she shared with me the specifics of her friend's suggestion.

"I don't know if I can make a change like that – it feels overwhelm-ing!" she blurted out, but she was also laughing.

"Maya, those feelings are totally appropriate and understandable." I offered as she sat down. "But I'm curious as to why you were laughing as you spoke to them just now . . ."

Maya stopped and raised her chin as she looked out the window. "I guess maybe I am just a little bit excited about the possibility." I opened my mouth to encourage her and she held up her hands and looked me straight in the eye with one raised eyebrow. "Just a *little* excited." I smiled. She would not let me rush her into something. She would use her Heart listening skill to tune in to her own inner truth before making any decisions. I knew in that moment that Maya was going to be just fine.

When I last connected with her, Maya was in an online sales training program with ScholasticSource Servicing, Inc., that she found challenging but much more enjoyable than she had at first expected. It turns out that Denise was right, and it was Maya who needed to see herself in a new way. She tells me now that "Working from home is nice. And the money is even nicer!"

Many of us of a certain generation (ahem) have faced this same challenge by degrees ourselves when it comes to the warp-speed trajectory of personal and business technology. Jobs that once required largely the "people skills" that Maya relied on suddenly demand the ability to learn software programs and keep up with their continual "upgrades". A worker's value to their organization is now impacted by how often they have to call tech support and whether they need a translator for that experience.

## The Coach's Perspective: Questions and Applications

1. Many, if not most, coach professionals are in the "transformation business", no matter the niche, the client issues, or the focus. What particular "status quo bias" do your clients typically struggle with? How are these biases reinforced by their listening habits?
2. Reinvention can pose many challenges for clients. Maya had social support and the Heart listening ability to tune in to her customers and create trust. What elements do you think need to be in place for a client to reinvent themselves professionally?
3. Our natural tendency to listen for reinforcement of what we already know – a kind of status quo bias – can get in the way of a client building new self-definition. Maya had to intentionally apply herself to tune in better to facts, data and systems – Head listening – in order to gain ground in a new profession. If you were training Maya for a data-saturated position, how would you help her gain the skills she needs in this area?

## You Might Try This . . . The Motivational Interview

The Motivational Interview has proven extremely effective in tackling substance abuse, problematic self perception, and behavioral change. *Psychology Today*[5] defines it as "a counseling method that helps people resolve ambivalent feelings and insecurities to find the internal motivation they need to change their behavior." This technique is particularly

effective at the beginning of a person's journey into coaching and counseling. As stress levels increase with the pressures on daily life, accessing
ways to amplify motivation toward needed change is a vital component
in helping a client progress.

Key to success in MI is deep and comprehensive Heart listening
skills: tuning one's ears toward the client's "change vs. sustain talk", and
eliciting their specific reasons for wanting to change. Then the focus of
the engagement can turn toward clearly defined next steps in achieving
specific goals based on a client's own perceptions and motivations.

Coaches, counsellors, and other mental health professionals can
often err on the side of "giving advice" – outlining and even assign-
ing actions the client should take on their own behalf. MI challenges
the practitioner to treat the client as an equal partner, to intentionally listen for evidence of a client's own motivation to change. MI has
been described as a guiding style that is midway between following
(reflective listening) and a more directive approach. Utilizing some of
the best elements of Heart listening, respect and genuine curiosity, MI
facilitates a natural flow of change based entirely on a client's motivation and autonomy.

Stephen Rollnick, PhD, and William Miller, in their book *Motivational
Interviewing: Helping People to Change (3rd edition),*[6] outline the
instances in a client's process where MI is particularly useful:

- When ambivalence is high and clients feel stuck in mixed feelings
  about change
- When clients have very little confidence in their capacity to make
  needed change
- When the benefits of change and disadvantages of a client's current
  situation are unclear.

Rollnick and Miller delineate the core foundational skills of Motivational
Interview technique as follows:

- Open questions to explore a client's experiences, perspectives, and
  ideas. Evocative questions offered in the Elicit-Provide-Elicit structure help the client discover and connect with their internal knowledge, motivation, and capacity for change. The coach can then seek

permission to offer their own knowledge of the issue and proceed to explore the client's response.

- Affirmation of strengths, efforts, and past successes amplify the client's confidence in their own ability to make change.
- Reflections based on deep and attentive Heart listening convey empathy and a genuine effort to understand what a client is talking about through repeating, rephrasing, or sharing a deeper guess about what the client is trying to communicate.
- Summarizing solidifies a shared understanding of what has been communicated and amplifies the most important information.
- Attending to the language of change tunes in to what is being said to deflect change (sustain talk) and to strengthen change (change talk).
- Exchange of information reinforces a mutually respectful partnership by speaking to the client's own expertise and skill in the journey toward change.

As I read through Rollnick and Miller's cogent work on MI, I am struck by how the technique resonates with the skills of Heart listening. Should you like to explore this technique further, I have done work as a trainer and a Standardized Client with the Health Education and Training Institute,[7] and their program is highly reputable. Other resources, programs,[8] and certification processes[9] are available both online and in person, should you like more information. Motivational Interviewing has wide applications in coach practice. Those who use it find it a valuable addition in empowering clients to create needed change.

# Heart Listening Modality Review: Section Summary

As a review of the Heart listening modality, let's revisit these aspects:

*Heart Listeners Listen for:*
- Emotional context
- Opportunities to build relationship and express empathy
- The truth beneath the words

- Vocalics, body language, facial expressions
- Timeframe: The present – what is happening right now

*Heart Listeners Are Curious About . . .*
- How someone really feels
- The emotional context that informs a situation
- The motivations that produce behavior

# Strengths and Challenges of Heart Listening

*Heart listening provides:*
- Information gleaned from subtle behavioral clues like facial expression, vocal tone, and body language
- Human perspective, empathy, compassion
- The ability to build relationships, partnerships, and alliance
- The ability to cultivate and nurture interpersonal trust
- Generous focus and attention to other's needs and priorities

*Heart listeners are challenged to:*
- Set personal and professional boundaries
- Focus and rely on information other than emotional
- Own and acknowledge unconscious biases

*Heart listener professions and industries (not a complete list)*

Education    Medicine    Social work    Journalism    Psychiatry
Travel    Non-profit leadership    Childhood development    coaching
Arts and culture    Humanities    Gerontology    Counseling

# Positive Intelligence Crossover With Heart Listening

## Saboteurs

**Pleaser** – Tries to gain acceptance and affection by rescuing, pleasing, often loses sight of one's own needs and can become resentful as a result.

**Avoider** – Extreme focus on the positive and pleasant. Often avoids difficult and unpleasant tasks and conflict.

## Sage Powers

**Empathize** – The compassionate ability to step into another's experience without judgement.
**Navigate** – Alignment with values, priorities, vision, a wider perspective.

# Balance and Amplify

If you recognize yourself in the Heart listening description and can relate to what I've depicted in these last stories, I invite you to consider how this modality might serve to reinforce a confirmation bias for you. Biases are emotional by nature, and they are there for a reason. They protect us from danger, they are a way to simplify our priorities, they help us define ourselves, and they may help us make sense of a chaotic world. But if we are too defended from what we don't recognize or understand, if we quickly dismiss what makes us uncomfortable simply because it doesn't align with what we already know, then we reduce our curiosity, and the walls around us grow stronger and higher.

If you suspect you or some of your clients are in the grip of a bias – and many of them are unconscious – I encourage you to experiment with the following activities:

- **Soften a bias:** Bring to mind a person who rubs you the wrong way. This person could be a colleague, a relative, someone you encounter on a regular basis. Take a deep breath and begin writing a letter or an email in their voice as if they were writing to you. Let them explain why they behave the way they do towards you. See where your imagination takes you, and notice if you might feel just a bit differently the next time you encounter them.
- **Shake up a habit:** Often change starts with one small consistent action. Drive to a destination using a different route, talk to a stranger, or try a new recipe. If you are used to dressing in grays, browns, and blacks, see how you feel if you add something red, orange, or pink to brighten things up.
- **See oneself differently:** If you work with clients like Maya, who are contemplating an important professional change, it can be difficult

for them to step into the unknown. I encouraged Maya to literally step into a new environment by asking her friend Denise to set up a site visit to the company. Clients with Heart listening as a primary modality are very able to tune in to the environment around them and to accurately gauge how a surrounding context will impact their wellbeing. During the pandemic, Maya did the majority of her work from home. Despite this, once her training was complete, she was able to discern much from that single visit: the interpersonal dynamics between employees, the engaged energy onsite, and the way people welcomed and encouraged her to get onboard. After that visit, Maya could more clearly see herself in a new role.

## For Clients Struggling With Heart Listening, Try This

*   **Identify the Obstacles:** What are the personal habits or circumstances preventing you from tuning in to your Heart listening? Are you always pressed for time? Feeling like you have to grab your phone or you'll miss something? Or do you struggle to take your focus off of what you will say in response to the person who's speaking to you? Prior to your conversation, take at least three deep breaths. Notice something in the environment you are in. Invite your conversation partner to share something off-topic that might set them more at ease. As they begin to speak, see if you can tune in to what is communicated beneath the words. Encourage them to open up about their authentic experience by inviting them to "Tell me more about . . ." (something they just said). Challenge yourself to simply listen without feeling the pressure to verbally respond.

**Probing Questions . . .** Often, Heart listeners enjoy answering many of these questions. Pay attention to the ones they struggle with, as their answers might reveal interesting layers in their experience.

1.  What keeps you in your occupation?
2.  How has it changed you?
3.  At the end of your life, what will you look back on that most mattered?

4. What scares you the most?
5. Who are your heroes?
6. What makes you feel successful?
7. Who do you trust the most right now? Why?
8. What makes you feel awe?
9. What feels most risky to you right now? How do you feel about that risk?
10. What belief/conviction would you like to let go of?
11. What makes a meaningful day for you?
12. Where do you feel most at home?
13. What do you feel is your best contribution to those around you?
14. How do you know when something is true?
15. What frustrates you the most when people communicate with you?
16. What's your preferred form of communication?
17. What are you most certain about?
18. What helps you learn/retain information the best?
19. Who/what has the most impact on you right now?
20. What have you recently discovered or learned that surprised you?
21. What challenges are you faced with right now?
22. What do you most like to do outside of work?
23. What do you do that lets you lose track of time?
24. What metaphors, if any, are you fond of using?
25. Please describe your optimum working environment

# Further Thoughts

If you've ever been surprised in a conversation by revealing much more about yourself than you may have intended, then you are most likely talking to a Heart listener. There is "something" about people who are skilled in this modality that sets others at ease and deepens the conversation. They elicit trust. They are not afraid to show vulnerability, and they honor it in others. As a country, as a species, we are truly in need of more Heart listening.

But there is a flip side to everything, and this modality can go overboard if there are not healthy boundaries in place. As we saw in Maya's story, skilled Heart listeners can become blinded to their own needs because of their focus on others. Additionally, confirmation biases of many kinds are rooted in emotion and the need to stay safe. Those with a very strong modality in Heart listening can be extremely powerful if they can find a way to utilize this skill and take action.

Action is what the next modality is all about.

# Notes

1 Social Capital: www.britannica.com/topic/social-capital
2 *Positive Intelligence Saboteur Assessment*, Chamine: www.positiveintelli gence.com/saboteurs/
3 *Positive Intelligence, the Pleaser*, Chamine: https://support.positiveintelligen ce.com/article/114-pleaser
4 *Positive Intelligence, Sage Qualities*, Chamine: https://support.positiveintelli gence.com/article/143-power-games
5 Psychology Today Definition of Motivational Interview: https://psychologyto day.com/us/therapy-types/motivational-interview
6 *Motivational Interviewing; Helping People to Change* (3rd edition), Rollnick, Stephen, PhD. and Miller, William
7 Health Education and Training Institute: www.hetimaine.org
8 Motivational Interviewing Resources: https://bit.ly/3tbGXqO
9 Certification Programs: https://bit.ly/3N6Kcb4

# PART

## 4

# Listening Styles: Hands Listening

## HAND LISTENING MODALITY:

### SECTION SUMMARY

**Hand Listener Professions and Industries**
(Not a complete list)

- Recruitment • Lawyer • Start-ups
- Journalism • Real Estate • Graphic Design • Travel • Sales • Lobbyist
- Medical and Legal Advocacy
- Experiential Learning
- Architecture • Landscaping
- Entrepreneurial Development
- Animal Training • Sports Training
- Tech Design • Interior Design
- Event Planner • Renewable Energy

**Hand Listeners Listen for:**

- Problems to solve
- Actions to take
- A map, a strategy
- New Possibilities
- Timeframe: The future

## POSITIVE INTELLIGENCE CROSSOVER

**Hand Listeners Are Curious about...**

- What hasn't been tried?
- What else might work?
- Workarounds
- The "how" in tackling a challenge

**Saboteurs**

- **Hyper Achiever:** Dependent on constant performance & achievement for self-respect & validation
- **Restless:** Constant search for greater excitement, new stimulation, constant busyness, rarely at peace or content with the current activity

## Benefits & Challenges

**Sage Powers**

- **Innovate:** Curiosity & exploration in creating new ideas & solutions
- **Activate:** The ability to take clear, focused action

**Hand Listening Provides:**

- Connections between ideas for new applications • Connections that build bridges between difference
- Multiple ways to consider a problem or issue • The ability to stay curious and follow internal promptings
- A healthy relationship to risk
- Adaptability & flexibility • Capacity to change direction when necessary

**Hand Listeners Are Challenged to:**

- Manage time • Manage distractions
- Prioritize activities towards a singular goal • Persevere through obstacles and difficulty • Identify and own their unconscious biases

# Hands Listening: The Problem Detective

When I first started in this work, I thought I was primarily a Heart listener. I'm empathic and tuned in to non-verbal messaging, but as I was developing the framework, my daughter was going through a difficult adolescence.

Each evening would find Rob and me on the back deck commiserating as she cried and complained. This kept up for a long time. I discovered that I actually have limited capacity for Hands holding. After a few weeks of the same sob stories, I lost a bit of patience and asked "Well. What can you *do about it*?" To which she replied "Mom! I just need you to *listen*!" Rob however, whom I knew to be a strong Head listener, with seemingly infinite capacity to just nod somberly, would hand her the tissue box and say, "Yeah, that sucks." I had assumed myself to be a much more empathic listener than my facts-and-figures husband. But apparently, I was mistaken. At least in this instance.

As a Head listener, Rob can often retain facts much better than I can, and he will seek out established precedents before undertaking a project, a trip, or a decision. This quality serves him and our family very well. It also affords him a degree of dogged patience in dealing with bureaucracy of any kind, and his research on home repairs, household decisions, and work opportunities ensures that we make choices that will benefit us long term. I'm glad to be partnered to someone with this listening modality, as my stores of this quality are unfortunately pretty low.

However, my problem-solving Hands listening keeps us from getting stuck in endless rounds of research, analysis paralysis, and information overload. Sooner or later we'll have to take action, and I am often the catalyst for much of it in our family. My modality gets us focused on finally

DOI: 10.4324/9781003296027-19

getting that new vacuum cleaner, fixing up the spare room for Air B&B rentals, or getting us out the door on an excursion to somewhere we've never gone. I'm better at taking risks that will expand our knowledge of where we are and what we can do. I'm good at coming up with a Plan B when Rob's Plan A falls to pieces. This often translates into my professional life. Clients know that I'm willing to experiment, try new things, and invent workarounds where necessary.

Let's identify some qualities that are distinctive to Hands listeners:

*Hands Listeners Listen for:*
- Problems to solve
- Actions to take
- A strategy
- New possibilities
- The future

*Hands Listeners Are Curious About . . .*
- What hasn't been tried yet?
- What else might work?
- Work-arounds
- The "how" in solving a problem

Hands listening is the most intentional and, arguably, improvisational of the modalities. This kind of listening is often used in finding connections between random elements, identifying new solutions, in innovative processes, in sales negotiations. The intention behind Hands listening is very clear: there is a tangible, practical, often measurable result. The Achilles heel for this modality is speed – often caused by something called the speed-thought differential. Most people speak at a rate of around 125 words per minute. But we have enough mental bandwidth to follow human speech at 400 words per minute. This means that when we listen to the average speaker, we use only about a quarter of our mental capacity.

For Hands listeners, then, we get caught in what Kate Murphy calls the "Yeah, yeah, I got it" syndrome,[1] which feeds our tendency to jump to conclusions. When I find myself doing this, I'm operating under the assumption that I understand and can predict what the speaker will say next. This annoying habit lessens my curiosity as well as my motivation to truly listen.

When there's a desired result at the end of the conversation, the combination of the speed-thought differential, the "Yeah, yeah I got it" syndrome, and high motivation throws some formidable road blocks into the path toward more effective listening.

If, however, you have ever witnessed seasoned sales people in action, you can bet that they have mastered these tendencies in order to produce high volumes of successful sales. Trevor's story is a good illustration of someone who has learned, through hard experience, to incorporate Hands and Heart listening into his sales relationships.

# Note

1    *You're Not Listening and Why It Matters*, Murphy, Kate, 2021

# Trevor's Story: Getting a Read on the Dream

Trevor, a greenhouse manager in his mid-40s, has worked in plant nurseries since he was in high school. He took his first summer job at Simmond's Lawn & Garden when he was 17. When he walked into the greenhouse that first day, he felt something inside him spring to life. The sizzling colors of the flowers in bloom, the pungent scents of soil and greenery, all began feeding a hunger he didn't even know he had. He went straight to the library after his shift ended and checked out every botany book he could find. By the time his summer tenure at Simmond's ended and his senior year of high school was about to start, he had become so proficient in learning the Latin names of the perennials and annuals, the succulents and specialty vines, and, perhaps more importantly, how to engage with customers while gaining their trust that the manager asked him to stay on as a permanent part-timer.

Earlier that year, Trevor had begun to suspect that he was not wired the same way as the other guys. By the time he started work at Simmonds, it was clear to everyone who knew him that he was gay. In a family of four brothers and an alcoholic father, living in a small rural community, Trevor was in for a rough time. His stoic silence at home brought on cruel teasing from his brothers – and the more than occasional beating from his dad. Trevor was determined to leave home as soon as he could. His mother begged him to consider attending college, as she was convinced he had "the brains" in the family, but the only way they could afford college tuition was if Trevor lived at home. That was a deal-breaker. College, as far as he could imagine it, wasn't going to happen.

However, as his circumstances at home darkened, Trevor's work life was gaining momentum. After his graduation from high school,

DOI: 10.4324/9781003296027-20

Simmonds was very happy to put him on full time, as he had become a favorite with the important customers the company relied on for repeat business. He seemed to have a knack for steering a client to longer-term, and more expensive, solutions to landscaping issues, regardless of what ideas they might have had when they began a conversation with him. As Millie Ferguson, an avid gardener and Simmonds customer of many years, exclaimed at the cash register one day "I came in for a couple of hostas, but here I am leaving with all these pricy conifers!"

Trevor smiled. "Millie, you're going to love them – they're gorgeous, healthy – and best of all – low maintenance. "And," he added, "You won't be constantly fighting off the deer!"

"I don't know, Trevor. " replied Millie. "I think you're working some kind of mumbo jumbo magic on us customers!" Knowing laughter bubbled up from the others waiting in line.

After Trevor had completed his first season of full employment, he'd saved enough to leave home while continuing his job with Simmonds.

When I first met Trevor, he was the perennial yard manager and the primary trainer of new employees. I could tell that he commanded respect from his team – most of them 20-something guys hired primarily for their physical strength, not their botanical interests. Whenever I would train with him, as I did for a time as part of my Master Gardener certification, I began to notice the way he became very still when talking with a customer. No matter what he may have been involved with at the time: taking inventory, loading an order for shipping, or managing a crew unloading a truck, he had the ability to slow himself down, come to a stopping place, and give his attention completely to the customer and their questions.

On a lunch break one day, I had a chance to talk with him about this ability.

"So Trevor, I have a question – and it's not about the plants."

Trevor laughed "Good!" It had been a very busy day in the greenhouse, with many impatient customers demanding his attention.

I continued. "I'm curious about this ability you have to slow yourself down, no matter what's going on around you, and really tune in to what a customer is saying to you. Do you practice meditation or anything like that?"

Trevor laughed again. "No way I'd ever be a meditator – I'm way too restless!"

"Me too." In fact, in the Positive Intelligence model, Restless[1] is my most prevalent saboteur. I persisted.

"I'm really struck by your ability to completely focus in these conversations you have with customers. Have you always been good at that? Or is it something you learned to do?"

Trevor shrugged. "I've never really thought about it, to be honest." Then he looked around the lunchroom and noticed we were alone. He turned back to me.

"But I kind of had to learn how to slow down and take the temperature of certain situations when I was growing up." He shrugged again. "You know, as a gay guy."

"Do you mean you were in danger somehow?"

"Oh yeah. Things could go south pretty quick around my house. School too."

Then he grinned. "But then I got a growth spurt and shot up to six foot four and they had second thoughts about pummeling me." I smiled too. We would tease Trevor about being a lightning rod when thunderstorms rolled through.

I wanted to know more. "But somehow, Trevor, you have managed to turn defensive awareness into a brilliant ability to engage with customers and make sales. How?"

Before he could answer that question, he was summoned to help yet another customer.

I decided to watch him that afternoon and to really focus on his behavior with customers, as well as those he worked with.

My first opportunity arrived in the form of a repeat customer known for being brusque with everyone. Everyone, that is, except Trevor.

"There you are!" Lillian announced, striding over to the table where Trevor had started to label the new lavender. Lillian Clayson-Pierce was born into, and married into, families of means with many properties around the state. She had put herself in charge of getting their newer property landscaped in time for her son's wedding. She is in her late 50s – tall, imperious, and in a state of constant urgency.

I saw Trevor take a deep breath before responding.

"Hey there, Lillian. How're things?" He turned from the lavender to look at her directly and gave her a bemused smile.

I watched Trevor engage with Lillian, known to the crew as "difficult" on the best of days. He gave her his full undivided attention and answered each of her questions slowly, oftentimes with a pause before he spoke. As I watched him, it seemed to me that he was mirroring Lillian's vocal cadences as well as her posture – both of which proceeded to soften significantly during their exchange. Lillian felt safe with Trevor. I wondered if this was an unusual feeling for her.

Trevor asked plenty of questions of course, and he stopped to truly absorb her answers. It became clear that he really was trying to get a sense of the overall vision that Lillian had for her property, along with the challenges present in that particular location. He spent the better part of an hour with Lillian. He showed her dozens of small trees and shrubs, explaining the benefits and growing habits of each. Lillian would express concerns and again, he turned fully towards her in answering her questions. The conversation was calm, deliberate, and respectful. He would crack a joke every so often, which elicited girlish laughter from Lillian. At the end of their time together, Trevor directed the crew to tag a large collection of maple trees, specialty pines, hydrangeas, grasses, and day lilies for pick up by her landscaper. This one sale alone had netted the greenhouse many thousands of dollars.

When I caught up to Trevor at the end of that day, I asked him about this conversation in general and, more specifically, what he had been listening for in dealing with Lillian.

"Well, I don't think I'm doing anything special," he said with a quizzical look on his face. "But now that you bring it up, I guess what I'm trying to do with customers is get a sense of what they're trying to build and why." He continued. "Like Lillian, you know. She's pretty tightly wound." We both rolled our eyes at that observation. "But this wedding is very important to her. And her long-term vision of the place needs to include stuff her future grandchildren would enjoy."

"Once I get a read on the dream, you could say, then I know how to advise them, and I can direct them to stuff that will really work for long-term investing in a healthy landscape."

I had never encountered that phrase "Getting a read on the dream" before, but I've come to understand that this is an important part of both Heart listening and active Hands listening. Why? Once you know the larger picture around what a customer, a patient, a client, or a "tightly wound" landowner is trying to accomplish, it can become the foundation on which you position yourself as an ally. You may remember that we discussed this in terms of the DEP experience earlier in the book.

## Some Questions You Might Ask Yourself in Teasing out the Dream . . .

- What's the most important change this person wants to make?
- What underlying need will that address?
- Can I relate and empathize with this need?
- Is there something I can offer that will address this need and result in better outcomes for all the parties involved?

This is information you will be able to gather by tuning in to your Heart listening in reading messages underneath the words and then applying that information to specific goals: Hands listening. It takes a degree of practice, patience, and intentionality, but, as I could see in watching Trevor, getting a sense of "the Dream" is critical to building trust in any interaction.

Additionally, Hands listening is very much a part of a communication technique called linguistic mirroring. This skill is illuminated and amplified with research into mirror neurons. When in conversation, if you can "mirror" your partner's communication style, you are more likely to be convincing in the engagement. The speaker comes away with a stronger sense of being listened to and understood more deeply.

It was truly an education to witness these skills in action as Trevor conducted his conversations with customers. I came to understand, too, the more I got to know him, that Trevor's empathic Heart listening skills were key to his effective and ethical Hands listening. Later in this chapter, we will briefly explore a notorious case where ethical Heart listening was left out of the practice of financial advising – with devastating impact.

## The Coach's Perspective: Questions and Applications

1. How might you apply effective Hands listening in building your own coach practice?

2. When watching someone else engage in conversation, how does mirroring show up in their interaction?
3. How do you apply mirroring when you engage in conversation with a client?

## You Might Try This . . . Vocal Mirroring

Maxim Sytch and Yong H. Kim, writing in the *Harvard Business Review* article titled "Want to Win Someone Over? Talk Like They Do",[2] suggest that to influence others, in a first conversation with a client, say, notice how they make sense of a situation, how they express their thoughts. What kinds of questions do they ask? How do they respond to your input? Then intentionally use this information in your own communication with them.

Sytch and Kim developed their framework by analyzing lawyers who wanted to influence the judges to which their cases were assigned. The following questions are ones included in their analysis. I have changed the language to better reflect coaching interactions.

Start by asking yourself the following questions when you next engage with a prospect or client:

1. In offering information to you as a current or potential coach, does this person gravitate towards facts and data or anecdotes and stories?
2. What kinds of information do they respond to best when you communicate with them?
3. When they speak to you, do they exude confidence and command, or do they exhibit a bit more humility?
4. Do they disclose personal information easily and early in the conversation? Or do they exhibit professional detachment? How hard do you feel you have to work to get them to open up?
5. Are the stories they tell ones that reveal any vulnerability?
6. When asking a question or answering yours, do they convey emotional energy, or are they calm and collected?

In addition to these questions, you might begin to notice how a person conveys themselves verbally. The better able you are to tune in to the "vocalics" the person uses in communicating: how fast they are speaking, how much pitch range they use, and match what you hear, the more successful the outcome of your conversation will be.

Linguistic mirroring is a great example of the combination of Heart listening skills; tuning in to non-verbal messaging, and Hands listening – utilizing this information while staying focused on the desired outcome and the issue that needs to be addressed.

# Notes

1   *Positive Intelligence*, Chamine: https://support.positiveintelligence.com/article/115-restless
2   "Want to Win Someone Over? Talk Like They Do", Sytch, M., Kim, Y.H., *HBR*, 2020

# Creativity: Data + Passion = Innovation

Though no one modality has a corner on creativity, effective Hands listening applies the history and data of the Heads modality with the emotional awareness of Heart listening. Hands listening will focus these kinds of information into a motivated, goal-oriented outcome. Often, it is this creative kind of listening required when facts and/or high emotion have run into a wall and something new needs to be tried.

But what is creativity? There are so many definitions! Here's what one person had to say about one foundational element of creativity.

JP Guilford, president of the American Psychological Association[1] for many years, voiced frustration with accepted explanations of our species' intellectual capacity. The overriding focus on *convergent thinking*: the quest to find the "right" answer, may be vital to our lives and our development, but Guilford was emphatic that our ability to invent *many possible answers* to the same question is also important. This ability, *divergent thinking*, would soon be considered a significant marker in creativity.

## Edi's Story: Out of the Blue, the Pink, the Yellow!

I discovered the following story of the mayor of Tirana, Albania, in the opening of Ingrid Fetell Lee's excellent book *Joyful*.[2] I include it here, as it provides an example of divergent thinking coupled with Hands listening to forge a creative solution.

Edi Rama was at a loss as to how to rejuvenate his community. Constricted for decades by a string of repressive dictatorships, life in Tirana

DOI: 10.4324/9781003296027-21

was starved of resources, devoid of motivation, and by 1999, suffering in the grip of crime and corruption. As he walked through his city, Rama saw gray concrete, gray skies, and gray stony faces. The mayor of Tirana was not a politician, an engineer, or an administrator. He was an artist. He began to pay attention to the few places, the corner cafe, the grocery, where there remained some splashes of color and design. He noticed in these places that voices became a little more animated, and as he tuned his ears to the emotional tone, he could almost discern, every now and then, a bit of laughter, a hint of joy, an attempted joke. These sparks were quickly extinguished once the exchange ended and the customer went back out into the dreary streets.

Rama decided to turn his observations into drastic action. He commissioned a painting service to paint a few buildings in the center of town in outrageous colors: bright orange, hot pink, sun yellow, sky blue. No explanation was given, but the effect was extraordinary: people were at first confused, some even a bit angry, but the mayor continued in his painting project. Unusual changes started to happen, slowly at first, then building in momentum. People began greeting each other and spending time in the public square, children attended school more regularly, citizens even picked up after themselves, and the chronic litter problem disappeared. Shop windows no longer were barricaded with metal gates, smiles became bigger and longer lasting. The only change made was the color of the buildings, but Edi Rama won the World Mayor Award in 2004 for the dynamic effect of this one application of creativity.

Hands listening is very often foundational to taking an untried action of some kind, to thinking "divergently", as happened in this case. Often, this listening modality is key in the discovery of new elements that can feed creative solutions to chronic problems. These could be on the individual level with client issues that have defied solutions so far, or with issues in self-perception, as we will see in the next chapter.

## You Might Try This . . . The Yes *And* Game

Before we move on, I'd like to share one of my favorite games as a way to help clients generate ideas to solve problems. In Edi's story, the low morale problem he saw in his fellow citizens was one that forced him to take a risk and apply what looked like a completely off-the-wall strategy: paint the buildings in startling colors. But your clients don't have to be artists to generate effective new ideas. This game comes from the Positive Intelligence model as part of the Innovate Sage power: The Yes *And* game.[3]

To have a successful game, you and your clients will need to understand the 10% rule: each idea offered in this game, no matter how whacky, has at least 10% validity. It is your job to find and articulate that 10%. Additionally, the language used in this game is very important, as you will see in the structure described here.

First, the problem needs to be clearly described. For example, perhaps a client is struggling with marketing their small business. You, as the coach, may want to ask for some specifics: are they trying to market a specific product or event? And so on. Once the problem is clearly stated, the game can begin.

Now, the client can offer something they have been considering, and the first offer is usually pretty realistic, like hiring a social media marketing person. Your job now becomes to find the 10% validity in that idea. You may know that this client's budget won't support hiring a quality social media person, but that fact does not enter the game. The 10% validity is all that is expressed. So the first thing you are required to say is "What I *like* about that idea is . . ." and then speak to the 10%, perhaps something like "I like that you are searching for help from sources outside your business. That way you can benefit from an outside perspective." This is the Yes part of Yes – And.

Next, you will need to come up with a different suggestion; it could be one that is connected to the client's first offer, but it doesn't have to be.

"I wonder if you might find some excellent help by hiring a college intern with social media skills".

Your client now needs to find and articulate the 10% with the same language. "What I like about that idea is . . ." And on you'll go, back and forth.

You will probably notice at a certain juncture that the ideas to that point have been pretty realistic. That's when you'll need to encourage a bit more risk taking, in yourself as well as your client. The 10% now becomes more challenging. "What if you were to run off a bunch of fliers advertising your product/event and hire some skydivers to jump out of a plane, tossing the fliers over the community you're trying to reach?" Your client knows this would be highly illegal in his location, plus it would be considered littering and not appreciated by his prospective customers, and it would blow his marketing budget for the year! Nonetheless, the 10% must be found.

"What I like about that idea . . ." And so on.

The point of Yes–*And* is to generate a large number of ideas and to push the envelope on what seems realistic and do-able. The usual ways to brainstorm are often limited to normal, familiar possibilities within budget constraints. The more whacky the ideas, the more we are challenged to find that tiny shred of validity, and the more energetic fun your participants will have while generating surprising solutions that also might be feasible. This game is particularly valuable in creating safe space for those offerings that might not have been mentioned at all without this structure.

When clients are resistant to finding the 10%, this is an interesting juncture. Oftentimes, we are habituated to listening for something *wrong* with an idea, so that we can elevate our status by diminishing the person who just put that whacky idea on the table. As a coach, you can find ways to gently steer the client's listening away from the obvious pitfalls of a suggestion, and towards the 10% value. The fact that Yes–*And* is a game, with rules and linguistic structure, helps shift participants away from their first negative response.

Note too that no one needs to say "I love that idea!", even if they do. The challenge is to tease out the 10%, speak to that only, and then offer the next idea.

I've used this game with individual clients, small groups of clients, and larger groups, in person as well as online. It never fails to shift perspectives from Problem to Possibility!

# Notes

1    "Creative Abilities in the Arts", Guilford, J.P., *Psychological Review*, 64(2), 1957
2    *Joyful*, Lee, Ingrid, 2018
3    *Positive Intelligence*, Chamine

# Ian's Story: Creativity in the Everyday

Ian is a partner in a small advertising agency. He sought coaching for help with what he called "creative blocks" that he felt were impeding his progress at work.

At our first meeting, Ian arrived on time, in a fully buttoned shirt, tie, and dark suit coat despite the sweltering temperatures outside. He said he had walked over to my office from a few blocks away, and he gratefully accepted the glass of cold water I offered him. Our session began.

Ian had been with the agency for about four years and had enjoyed his job. "Well", he said, and hesitated. "Certain elements of it, anyway."

"Tell me more about those elements, Ian." This was our first encounter, and I wanted to get a sense of what he enjoyed about his job and what he considered his strengths.

"Well, I like the intake sessions with the client."

"And what is it about those sessions that you enjoy?"

"I really like listening to the give and take with the client – the messages they want amplified, the problems they want solved, the numbers they want to hit. The entire team gets into the Q&A. I mostly listen and try to get down all the data so that I can crank out a spreadsheet to inform our next session." He paused to take a sip of water.

I discovered in this conversation that I had some assumptions about the advertising profession that were informed largely by *Saturday Night Live* brainstorms – fueled by pizza and lots of beer. I was about to be reeducated.

"I like quantifying the elements of a session and doing the outside research so that we can really give the client what they want." We hadn't gotten to the Listening Assessment yet, but Ian was sounding like a Head listener.

DOI: 10.4324/9781003296027-22

"So, Ian, I'm hearing that you have a particular skill set that your agency finds very useful. Your ability to quantify largely qualitative information in a conversation and representing that quantitatively and visually is fascinating. I don't think I imagined that process as part of building an ad campaign."

Ian shrugged and grinned sheepishly. The first non-professional smile I'd see so far. "Not many people do consider the importance of data crunching in this business."

Now that he was feeling acknowledged and affirmed, it was time to dive into the issues that brought him in.

"So what brings you in to see me today, Ian?"

I watched his face fall. He sat up straight in his seat, squared his shoulders, looked out the window behind me and shifted the conversation.

"I'm in a highly creative industry." He swallowed hard. "And I'm just not very creative."

This highly competent, skilled professional had just pronounced a sentence on himself.

The silence sat there in the room. I let it sit for a bit.

It's unfortunate what western cultures historically have done to creativity. It gets put into its box, labelled as frivolous, artsy, fun, and largely useless or, conversely, placed upon a high pedestal to be accessed by only the chosen few.

I was greatly saddened by Ian's harsh assessment of himself. It was clear that the messaging of his internal Judge would have to be patiently questioned and dismantled.

I cleared my throat. "Ian, I'm going to table that statement for the moment, but we will get back to it later. Right now, I'd like to ask you about something else."

Ian took a deep breath and looked directly at me as if he were going to be interrogated. "Of course, go ahead."

"Was there a specific event that made you decide to seek coaching outside the company? What was it that made you want to get some help?"

"Well." He shifted in his seat. "We have a new client on board, [a large global retailer specializing in outdoor apparel] and, because we have some people out sick, the pressure is on for all of us, including me, to pitch in with the creative ideas." He looked down at the table in front of him. "I can't hide behind the spreadsheets anymore. I have to come up with some creative ideas and I'm just drawing a blank – like I don't know how to do this part." He looked directly at me, and his voice took on a frustrated edge I hadn't heard so far as he continued. "And that's ridiculous! I mean, for God's sake, I'm in advertising!"

"Ian," I responded, "Everyone has creativity. Yours has simply gone underground for awhile. Let's get it back, shall we?"

Once I gave Ian the Listening Modality Assessment, it was clear that Ian was a Head listener, but he had very strong scores in Hands listening as well. Again, Hands listening is informed by both Head and Heart modalities and is very helpful in bringing creativity into problem solving. Ian's self perception appeared to be a problem.

"Ian, I'm curious about what associations you have with the word 'creativity'. What does that word bring up for you?"

He took a deep breath and thought for a moment. "Well, I associate creativity with the people I work with."

"Okay, and why is that?"

"Well, they always seem to be playing around with ideas – bouncing stuff off each other – lots of storytelling and that kind of thing."

"Storytelling?" This was a piece of specificity that could prove interesting to dig into.

Ian smiled a bit ruefully. "Yeah, they're always coming in with stories about their lives at home, you know, funny stuff the kids did, or whatever."

"And do those stories ever make their way into a campaign?"

Ian looked taken aback. "Well . . ." He stopped. "Sometimes?" He looked out the window. "I guess they do, actually. Not often, but sometimes."

"And Ian, do you share your own stories at work?"

He was back to shifting in his seat. "I try." He looked down.

"Okay . . . ?" He wasn't going to give me more without my prompting him. "So what happens with those stories, Ian?"

He shrugged. "It's hard for me. I get a little lost in the details, and somehow I lose the point of the story." He looked down and away, and I saw his shoulders sag.

I reassured him that this was a very common pitfall for many people trying to tell stories. It's as if they feel they do the listener a disservice if they leave any of the facts out of the telling. But facts are not really the point of a story, are they? The purpose of a story is to make us feel something – like that wonderful quote attributed to Maya Angelou: "People won't remember what you said. They won't remember what you did. They will remember how you made them feel." This means we need to pick and choose the facts we need in order to make the story "sing".

"Ian, I want to prove to you that you can tell a story." His eyes widened. "Well . . . Okay . . ." But he looked very unsure.

I wasn't certain how to start, but I dove in anyway. "Tell me about something out of the ordinary you did over the last few weeks." Ian's eyebrows came together, and he looked a little incredulous. "Why would you want to know about something like that?"

I smiled. "Honestly? I'm not sure. But humor me, okay?" He shrugged, and thought about it for a bit, and then began to tell me the story that follows.

Ian had been asked by his wife to drive up north to a small coastal town and pick up a large load of seaweed. "She wanted to put some seaweed in the garden as mulch. She needed a lot of it, apparently, so I drove our pickup there last Saturday. It's a ways up the coast. It took about three hours to find the place."

"Good start, Ian. What happened next?"

I watched him shift again in his seat. Then he took a sip of water. "Uhm. I found the place okay, and the guy at the entrance told me to drive my truck right out onto the pier. So I did that. Then I realized I wasn't the only guy waiting there." Ian stopped and looked out the window. I sensed the story was about to change.

"Who else was there at the dock?"

"There were about five guys there. Big fisherman type guys in waders and rubber boots. They were all kind of talking to each other and I guess they were waiting on a boat that was about 500 yards out."

Then he stopped. "Actually, it was more like 900 yards out or so."

This was one of the junctures I was waiting for. "Ian, is the yardage important to the story you are telling?"

"Oh." His eyes travelled around the room. "I guess . . . not."

I smiled. "Then you can leave it out. That's one of those details you were talking about before, right?"

He looked sheepish again, and smiled. "Right."

"So how did you feel, realizing you wouldn't be the only one waiting for the boat?"

He laughed a little. "Well, I suddenly realized that I had worn all the wrong stuff."

"How so?"

"I had had a meeting at church before I drove up there, and I was wearing my chinos and a blazer and my leather loafers."

My turn to laugh. "Oh! Right. That's a pretty vivid picture Ian. And how did that make you feel?"

"Like an idiot." He was laughing now. "I didn't even want to get out of my truck!"

Suddenly I realized something.

"Ian. Tell me if I'm right about this." I was not sure where this would lead, but I was curious nonetheless. "A good marketing campaign needs to address some pain point for the consumer, right?"

Ian looked quizzical and nodded.

"So, what I hear in your story is a pain point for a guy who is not wearing the right outdoor gear in this very particular environment – right? And the peer pressure is pretty palpable – and relatable – yes?"

Suddenly, Ian's face lights up. "Wow!" He laughs. "I never would have thought to connect that story with a client campaign."

"Not true, Ian." I'm laughing now, too. "Because you just did!"

If you follow the process of Ian's discovery in this chapter, you can see that he began with the Head-gathered facts of his experience. I then urged him to go a bit deeper to name his Heart-centered feelings. And after those two elements are identified, the creativity of Hands listening can be activated.

As a reminder, Head listening is concerned with the past: facts and patterns that have been proved and established. Heart listening is focused on the present: what is happening now, what the emotional reality is in the present moment. Hands listening applies both those elements toward the future: how to make use of what is accessed through both these modalities toward a specific goal.

I'd like to offer two more observations before we move on from Ian's story, and the first one has to do with how popular culture can often replace our own ability to imagine. Think about the last time you read a novel; you populated it with the places and faces of people in your imagination. Then you go to see the movie made of the same story. Those faces and places you conjured up have now been replaced forevermore by

Hollywood's choices. This may seem trivial, but think about the impact, over time, of a nation's reduced ability to imagine. The "failure of imagination" in heading off the 9–11 disaster is only a single vivid example of the horrendous cost. We downplay the importance of imagination at our own peril.

The second observation has to do with Ian's all-too-common assumption that personal, real-life stories don't have much value outside of our own small circles. In my experience, nothing could be further from the truth.

We often don't think of our own stories as creative fodder. In contrast to Netflix, Hollywood, and all the sensationalized news we are fed on a daily basis – our personal everyday stories can seem pretty tame and mundane, but they are not. They are our source of connection to each other. They are lifeblood for our souls, our psyches, and maybe even our sanity.

Now, of course, with all the ubiquitous posting on social media by those who are convinced their every move is fascinating, personal stories can become cheapened simply because they are flying at us from every channel. Nevertheless, the look of sheer delighted discovery on Ian's face when I offered him an opportunity to bridge his story with his work challenge tells me that I'm on the right track.

Transforming the stories clients tell themselves about who they are and what they are capable of is key to a successful coach process. Then there are those situations, as we will see in the next chapter, where a client struggles to transform their professional story in the face of stubborn and intractable cultural assumptions.

I continued to work with Ian on a variety of ways to access and tell personal stories, some of which I'll share in the "You Might Try This" section of this chapter.

# The Coach's Perspective: Questions and Applications

1. How do you address a client's attitude toward their own creativity?
2. How might you apply storytelling as a skill with certain clients?

3. How do you begin to dismantle the negative self assumptions clients struggle with?

4. What's an example in your own coach practice where you helped a client change the story they are telling about themselves?

5. How can we, as coaches, help clients better use their own imaginations in their journeys toward self-actualization?

# You Might Try This . . . The Five Ingredient Story

For clients who struggle with effective storytelling because, like Ian, they want to make sure they get all the facts and details in, I've been experimenting with the Five Ingredient Story. (You've probably found food metaphors to be useful in working with clients too.) The beauty of this story form is the requirement to hone the story down to not more than five essential elements. So for Ian's seaweed trip, I had him write the story in paragraph form, with only five sentences, using these questions:

1. **What needs to be accomplished?** His wife needs seaweed for her garden.

2. **How did you accomplish this?** Ian drives his truck up the coast to a small fishing town.

3. **What's the obstacle?** Ian is very uncomfortable with being the only guy on the pier not dressed like a fisherman.

4. **What's the result?** He gets his seaweed, but has to endure the stares of the locals.

5. **What's the learning?** Ian now has a pair of large rubber boots and a hunting vest in the truck just in case he finds himself in this kind of situation again!

There are other models of this same form. I've used the Three Ingredient Story with clients as an alternative to memorizing their elevator speech. The three ingredients in this form are:

1. **Something about who you are:** This is an invitation to authenticity – something true and even relatable that you can share about where you are: in life, in your job – not just your title.

2. **Something you've done:** Now we're talking about credibility – What's your most recent success? Let yourself get excited about it.
3. **Something about what you want:** A Call to Action with a difference. What really rings your chimes and would make your month if you could get it?

I work with clients who are often at the beginning or in the middle of their careers or have to take on a career change. When I introduce the Three Ingredient Story as an alternative to the elevator speech, often clients respond with relief! Why? Because the Elevator Speech can feel "canned" and sales-y, whereas the Three Ingredient Story is an opportunity to share authenticity, accomplishment, and an enthusiastic Call to Action that hits the informational marks while creating a stronger emotional connection in response to the question "What do you do?"

# You Might Try This . . . The Story Walk

This technique was shared with me years ago by the late, great improvisation teacher David LaGraffe – someone I consider the "Buddha of Improv". He will be forever missed by those of us fortunate enough to have worked with him.

Encourage your client to give themselves a free afternoon. Have them take a pen and notebook with them as they start walking from one part of town or any rural setting of their choice to another. Have them stop at certain junctures, say, every 15–20 minutes, and tune in to what their senses are telling them. Encourage them to write down these observations. If they enjoy drawing, encourage this as well. Note that they are to pay special attention to what they hear. For example, right now, I'm hearing the gurgle of the water in a small fountain on my deck. I'm also hearing a jet flying overheard, traffic a block away, a catbird and a blue jay. How do these sounds make me feel? What do I notice that I haven't heard before? What changes as I continue to listen?

Once these observations have been made, they are free to walk for another span of time, then sit and make observations.

Even one hour of this exercise has many benefits: people report a slowing down of their heart rate, a feeling of being in tune with one's environment, and a deeper interest in what is going on around them. For those who struggle with ADHD, this single exercise can give clients a palpable sense of what can be gained by slowing down, paying attention without judgement, and expanding our perception into whatever there is to be discovered in the world around us.

# Ruthie's Story: Listening to the Internal Voice

I first encountered "Ruthie" when a friend suggested I step into her small shop and gallery. I don't know what I expected to see, but what I was not expecting was to enter a clean well-lit space populated entirely with very unusual chairs: chairs made from truck tires, chairs created exclusively out of large ceramic flowerpots, chairs fashioned from clothesline and swinging lazily from the ceiling. Everywhere I looked in Ruthie's shop, I saw objects designed for one utilitarian function creatively and delightfully transformed into a completely different utilitarian function. Need a handbag created out of recycled potato chip bags? No problem! How about a coatrack anchored by old leather boots at the base, holding up a section of PVC pipe with antlers attached to the top shellacked with multiple layers of brass paint? Or maybe a water fountain for the patio made from metal pie tins and colorful plastic funnels to serve as water conduits? As I wandered around this amazing place and took in the painstaking detail that went into the design of these wonderful creations built from everyday repurposed objects, I realized that there was more at work here than creative whimsy – Ruthie had real engineering chops.

After I purchased a potato chip handbag (I was tempted by the coatrack but . . . it was maybe just a bit too showy for me), I got to talking with Ruthie. Before she emigrated to the United States, Ruthie had been an architecture student in her homeland of Nigeria. Once she arrived in the states and had gone through the mandatory waiting period to apply for US citizenship, Ruthie struggled to find employment. She worked part time in a chicken processing plant and as a housekeeper in a large hotel chain. Over the course of 15 years, through many changes and challenges, Ruthie kept creating.

DOI: 10.4324/9781003296027-23

"I would ride the bus every day – to school, or to work, and see so many sad homeless people, just nowhere to go, nothing to do with themselves. And I'd see trash on the street – an old bucket, a coat hangar – just thrown away, and think 'there's still life in that thrown away thing! Just like there is still life in those sad thrown away people!'"

She stopped then and let me take that in for a second. Her gaze shifted to the window facing the street.

"So one day, a summer day, I decided to walk home from work at the chicken plant. I had a shift that ended around noon, so after I ate my lunch, I began walking back to where I lived. It was a long walk, maybe ten miles or so."

Ruthie stopped then to ring up another sale. The bell on the door rang as the customer stepped into the street.

I asked her then "Ruthie, what made you decide to walk home on that particular day?"

She flashed a dazzling smile at me, threw her head back and laughed. "I didn't know! It was so crazy of me! And when I got home, my feet were so sore!

Then her face transformed into a fascinated expression.

"But all that morning, as I was working, I would have this thought – like a voice inside me telling me 'Ruthie! You should walk home today – you should walk home!' It was very insistent! So I listened. I walked all the way home. And along the way, I had found many objects just thrown in the street: a keyring, a lampshade, a mattress with springs popping out of it, just waiting for me to snatch them up! And just when I couldn't carry any more things in my arms, I see a huge shopping bag rolling toward me on the wind!" Ruthie laughed again, and her whole body shook with joy.

"I kept seeing these things along the way, and gathering them up. I didn't even know why, at first." She laughs again. "I have a very small apartment! No room to put all of these crazy things! But as I was putting them into the bag . . ." She stopped then and looked at me seriously. "You will think I'm crazy."

I assured her I wouldn't think that, and I encouraged her to continue.

She took a deep breath. "As I was gathering these things, ideas of what to do with them would start to come into my head, like the objects themselves were giving me ideas of how they wanted to be used! And I saw suddenly that I was to give them – these thrown-away-into-the-street things, I was to give them a new use, a new home – like those boots!" She pointed to the coatrack. "And all that clothesline!" – the one she had transformed into the chair swinging from the ceiling.

"I felt, as I walked, something coming alive inside of me, like something had been asleep a long time and was finally waking up!"

Ruthie turned her attention to another customer who was interested in a pair of lamps with reclaimed bucket lampshades. I noticed a newspaper article framed on the wall behind the register. Apparently, Ruthie had been the winner of a national competition for artists to submit designs for public spaces. Her "Child's Play" rendering of a seasonally evolving playground had won her a $35K prize! The article was dated two years prior and had launched Ruthie into the national artistic spotlight.

She returned to the counter and noticed me reading the article. She laughed her joyous laugh. "Oh, yes! That made me kind of famous for awhile. I could quit all my other jobs, and the money helped me start my store!"

I glowed inside for the rest of my day, simply from having encountered such an inspiring story from this generous, delightful, and resilient human being.

Ruthie was not a client of mine, but I include her story here for a number of reasons.

Anyone who coaches or counsels those in various resettlement programs will recognize the struggle, creativity, and resilience in Ruthie's story. Risking all to relocate in an unfamiliar culture often erases one's professional life – everything that once endowed a person with status, definition, and self esteem.

To rebuild one's life in a foreign country, and to flourish among strangers in a strange land, an immigrant like Ruthie has had to strengthen her Hands listening skills in many situations. To be able to adapt to radical changes in language, culture, and climate requires an amplified ability to quickly pivot and extend one's perceptual radar in order to make sense of new surroundings. This is a journey that would challenge the best among us. Our culture would benefit greatly if we could but acknowledge and honor those who appear, sound, and act differently from those who are native born. Most of us have no experience of what immigrants and refugees have endured.

Additionally, Ruthie exhibits the essence of Hands listening when it comes to creativity and innovation. As an architecture student, she listened and absorbed the facts and proven principles she needed to apply to her chosen profession. When she arrived in the States as an immigrant, she was not able, initially, to put these skills to use. But she knew how to listen to the clear prompting of her internal voice and could follow it into unfamiliar territory. Further, she could then tune in to her internal Hands listening to capture ideas in how to utilize random found objects in constructing her creations.

As we've seen in Maya's story in the Heart listening section, there is an element of Hands listening that allows us to tune in and listen to one's internal voice, especially when applied to creativity and problem solving. We are, by now, familiar with the notion of pondering a problem, a challenge, a decision during our waking hours, only to wake up with the solution front and center in our minds. Many of us have experienced this, though maybe not as frequently as we would like. It could very well be that there are elements of Hands listening in this process. As one works diligently during waking hours to find answers, the groundwork is progressing, but that effort is not enough. There still needs to be an internal alignment that allows the disparate elements to "click" into place. Being receptive to intuitive internal voice is, I believe, key to this process.

Ruthie's daily bus ride afforded her opportunities to notice the landscape she traveled through. Each day she "collected" information along the route: the homeless people, the discarded detritus. These trips inspired both empathy and a sense of possibility in what most of the rest of us would consider waste. This was Ruthie's "research"; this was the groundwork she laid internally. Then came the moment when her internal voice spoke loudly to her to bypass the bus and walk home. No explanation was given, but Ruthie followed this prompting, and her life changed dramatically as a result.

In many ways, Ruthie's story can also be considered an example of fortuitous serendipity. But before we simply label Ruthie one of the "lucky" ones, let's dig a little deeper into what constitutes serendipity.

Christian Busch, PhD, in his book *The Serendipity Mindset, the Art and Science of Creating Good Luck*,[1] describes serendipity as a continual process of "connecting the dots" in our experiences: of staying curious and open to changing circumstances and actively laying the groundwork so that new opportunities can be grasped. This "connecting the dots" in serendipity is also a key component of an effective Hands listening experience.

In Busch's description of "thunderbolt serendipity",[2] there is definite resonance with Ruthie's Hands listening. Thunderbolt serendipity "follows something entirely unexpected, like a thunderbolt in the sky, and sparks a new opportunity, or solves a previously unknown problem. We often fall in love this way, and many new ideas and approaches emerge."

I reconnected briefly and by accident with Ruthie when our country was in the throes of the shutdown. She had decided to close her wonderful shop, as business had slowed to a crawl and the owner of the building had increased the rent substantially. Ruthie was working on her résumé to try to position herself as someone with engineering skills so that she could gain employment in the construction industry, but getting past the initial submission and into an interview was very challenging. She'd had no luck in eight months of trying. The sparkle had gone out of her eyes. She told me, after our initial (masked and distanced) greetings, that she was worried she would once again have to board the bus for shifts at the chicken processing plant.

I asked her then, "Ruthie, have you been able to connect with any customers of your shop about possibilities? Anyone who might be connected in the business community?"

"Yes, I have tried to do this." Ruthie shook her head. "But still no interviews." I watched her shoulders sag. "One of them told me that her company wasn't in a position to hire artists." She then looked off into the distance and her voice took on a harder edge. "It's like everyone gets put into boxes here in this country. So because I won a contest with a playground design and had a shop for awhile selling silly things, then my value is only as an artist." She sighed. "Making silly things."

Ruthie's frustration is real. And it is shared by many creative and innovative problem solvers, along with those considered "on the spectrum". Business communities large and small have done themselves, our country, and a workforce with valuable and essential skills a huge disservice by refusing to step outside the boundaries of their preconceived notions about what constitutes an employable candidate, as well as their reluctance to invest in appropriate training.

Ruthie and I exchanged phone numbers. I thought about her history, her skills, and the strange shutdown circumstances we were now all of us enduring. As I took my daily walks in my suburban neighborhood, it occurred to me that I was seeing more children out in the streets, more cars in the driveway. The schools, of course, had shut down. The kids were stuck at home, and parents, those who could, were working from home. Families were all cooped up together . . . at home. Hmmm.

I called Ruthie with a suggestion. Perhaps she could offer, starting with her former shop customers, a service in at-home playground design? The delight in her voice at my suggestion brought tears to my eyes.

This new direction would not be easy, of course. Even if she managed to secure contracts, Ruthie would have to find workers to help build the structures, she would have to somehow gain scarce materials, she'd have to learn to market herself in this new venture. From what I know of Ruthie, though, she is very much up to the task.

As coaches with clients who struggle, for a wide range of reasons, to gain employment, this frustration with the "boxed and labelled" hiring practice of so many businesses is a constant and resounding theme. For coaches in the executive space, it can be challenging to help their clients widen their perspective enough to include potential employees outside of a very narrow range of traits, work history, and skill. But this is work well worth doing and can result in significant benefit for both businesses, customers, and their surrounding community.

## The Coach's Perspective: Questions and Applications

1. How might building sensory awareness help your clients?
2. How do you encourage greater sensory awareness in your own work?
3. Clients may, like Ruthie, struggle to gain employment that puts their best skills to use. How would you go about helping them?

## You Might Try This . . . Rename the Object

This is an interesting, and quite challenging, exercise that I have found to be effective in encouraging clients and students to gain awareness of rigid definitions of "reality" and experience in shaking them up. This activity is best approached in the spirit of play!

Encourage your client to walk around the room and just look at what is there, for example: a desk, a window, a lamp, a chair. Then ask them to point at random objects in the room, but assign them a different name and speak that name out loud. For example, the client might point to a potted plant and say "radio", or a window could become a dog, and so on. Once they've done this renaming a dozen or so times, debrief the exercise with some questions:

1. How did that activity make you feel? Responses may vary from "stimulated!" to "frustrated!" to "It's giving me a headache!"
2. Did your answers fall into a certain category, like foods, animals, or objects that start with the letter "R"?

Ask them to repeat the pointing and renaming exercise, but this time, encourage them to take a deep breath before naming the object. Observe any differences in how they rename the objects: tone of voice, energy, and so on. Debrief with questions about how they feel about that experience and what differences they may have noticed.

Again, approaching this exercise in the spirit of play is essential! Otherwise, it just seems like a pointless random brain-cramp. The objective here is to create an experiential awareness of how strong our labelling associations are and how difficult it is to shake them up. This can also work as an experiential linguistic metaphor for creating empathy with those who enter our country with no knowledge of our language, customs, and way of being. Additionally, speaking the alternative label aloud creates, at first, cognitive dissonance, which is pretty uncomfortable for most people. But after awhile, and with, again, the spirit of play, clients have often come away with a feeling of lightness and possibility – like discovering the world anew.

You might try this exercise in couples therapy as well. Two people re-labelling out loud simultaneously in the same space will be experienced as chaotic at first, with, again, a wide range of reactions. But once they gain greater facility, you might encourage them to see if they can build an alternative "world" together. I once did this exercise with two people who began labelling in separate categories: she was renaming largely within the category of water and the ocean, her partner was label-ling primarily in household utilities. When I encouraged them to begin to listen to each other's categorical labelling and to intentionally build a linguistic bridge: together they eventually created a submarine!

## You Might Try This . . . The Deep Seeing Exercise

This activity is included in Sarah Stein Greenberg's fascinating book *Creative Acts for Curious People*.[3] I include it here as a means of sharp-ening the awareness of what our senses are processing around us all the time. Right now, in this moment, you are processing the words on this page, but beneath your awareness, you may also be: seeing your partner cooking a meal in your peripheral vision, feeling an odd itch on your shin, hearing traffic outside the window you are sitting next to, and so on. Only a tiny fraction of what goes on around us all the time is actually registered in our consciousness. Our brains are actively protecting us by filtering what we are consciously aware of. It is Stein-Greenberg's assertion that we can control this filter and learn to pay better attention to what is right in front of us. The activity she describes[4] is focused on visual sensing. I have added an adjustment for auditory observation.

Encourage a client to do the following exercise once a day and to consider keeping a journal or a log to document observations.

Visual sensing: Use a real-life photograph, one where there are a number of things going on, multiple people, objects, and so on. A street scene would work well for this. Assign these questions once the photo-graph is chosen.

What's going on in this picture?
What do you see that makes you say that?
What else do you see?
What do you see that makes you say that?

Then repeat the process. Every day. This process opens a window into deeper understanding of how much detail is in our daily experience. It also encourages us to look at the stories we create around what we see and how our imagination fills in gaps in our observations.

## This Same Exercise Can Be Utilized for Deeper Listening

Have your client listen to a section of a recording: a podcast, an interview, or a segment of a radio play. The same routine applies here: daily listening, documenting what is heard, and noticing the depth of observations as they add up through the week. Encourage your client to tune in to the associations they may make about tone of voice, rate of speech, repeated words or phrases, and the effect of what is heard on their own sensibility and frame of mind.

*You might include these questions as a way into this experience:*
What's going on in this recording?
What do you hear that makes you say that?
What else do you hear?
What do you hear that makes you say that?
And so on.

Clients will often show up to their next session very surprised about what they had not noticed in their daily listening and/or viewing. At the very least, this is an exercise that builds awareness about our mental filters: how they serve us, as well as how they prohibit us from really noticing our everyday world.

## A Cautionary Note About Hands Listening

Hands listeners are challenged by a perceived lack of time. Our to-do lists are crammed already, and yet we are tempted to squeeze more in. Those in time-impacted professions like medicine can make costly and dangerous decisions in an effort to save time: not asking open-ended questions that may reveal critical information about a patient or accepting her story about that facial bruise despite her inability to make eye contact.

I know that if I'm not conscious and intentional, I find my listening is confined to the surface information I could get more quickly by email. This impacts the quality of my listening as well as the choices I make around it, which is why I have chosen to share the following story.

Paisley needed walking, and so did I. For both human and dog, it's not so much a walk as a daily "march" relegated to a half hour and no more. This schedule, fortunately, works for us both.

On a particular afternoon prior to the 2020 election, we turned onto the walkway that took us into the park. And there, on the park bench, sat an unusual visitor. An elderly man and a small French bulldog, enjoying the September sunshine. On the man's head was a brand-spanking new MAGA hat declaring "Trump–Pence in 2020!" His presence felt like a challenge here in this very liberal east coast small town. I realized I had an opportunity that I have talked about many times but not actually encountered. I could ask the man some questions about why he supported this president. I could engage in conversation with someone from the opposite side of the political spectrum and find out the story that fuels his point of view. Yes, here it is.

And yet . . .

My mind rifled through my schedule this afternoon. What could fall off? How long would I have to sit and talk with a stranger about politics? What if we got into it and it took more than the 30–45 minutes I had for this walk? And of course, there would be no walk. And my dog needed her walk. We moved on.

I've often thought back to that missed opportunity. Was I afraid to talk to this man? I can honestly say no. It was broad daylight in a public place, and he had a very cute, well-cared-for dog. I'm not usually reticent to talk to strangers, and no one finds me particularly threatening. The reason I took a pass was my perceived lack of time. This saddens me. We Americans make this same choice every day, and by doing so, we continue to calcify the divisions that tear our country apart. Bridging division is what the next chapter is all about.

# Notes

1    *The Serendipity Mindset*, Busch, Christian, 2020
2    *The Serendipity Mindset*, Busch, page 23
3    *Creative Acts for Curious People*, Stein Greenberg, Sarah, 2021
4    *Creative Acts for Curious People*, Stein Greenberg, page 64

# Craig's Story: Make Shift Coffee House

I have entered a large room in the town hall building of a small community in Maine. I'm surprised by how packed the place is. People sit at circular tables chatting rather tentatively with those sitting nearby. I see signs posted saying "Please sit with someone you don't know!" That explains the careful conversational tone. Bulletin boards surrounding the crowd are filled with small pieces of paper, headlined with "Share a Label You Have Experienced." Some of the labels include "Flakey Artist", "Dumb Housewife", and "Stupid Redneck". Also "The Boss" and "From Away".

I've arrived at my first Make Shift Coffee House (MSCH).[1] MSCH is a nationally acclaimed effort to get people talking to each other across difference on topics that impact our culture. Tonight's topic is "Labels". What labels have you been carrying? How do you feel about them? What labels do you attach to others, and why?

Craig Freshley, of Good Group Decisions,[2] begins the conversation by speaking about labels and their impact on our self-assessment. He will also address our tendency to label others – a kind of shortcut we take to find out whether someone is a potential friend – or not. He then invites those in attendance to speak about their own experience of labels. There are stories of being labelled wealthy and therefore "greedy", stories of living middle class and being labelled "poor". The musician in the room feels rankled about being labelled "lazy". A high school teacher reacts to the adage "Those who can – do. Those who can't – teach". Story after story illustrates the resentment and emotional shut-down that results from being labelled in our culture.

Craig encourages each of us to participate in small table groups and to share our experiences with our table mates. I sit next to a staunch

DOI: 10.4324/9781003296027-24

conservative Republican tired of being automatically classified as a Trump supporter and a self-proclaimed socialist who complains about being labelled a "Commie Pinko".

The Make Shift Coffee House model is deeply committed to the sharing of personal stories to invoke empathy and understanding and to encourage interpersonal connection in order to grow our capacity to listen with our hearts. This might be familiar to some as similar to the impetus around "deep canvassing"[3] – a method that promotes candid two-way conversations between canvassers and voters to get them to share the experiences that form their views. This method has proven 102 times more effective in shifting voter choice than the usual political campaign. In both deep canvassing and MSCH, the foundational premise is that if enough of us truly employ our Heart listening with someone we disagree with, *and make them feel truly heard*, we will be able to bridge the seemingly intractable chasms that divide our nation. Deep canvassing is explored a bit more in the final chapter of this book.

Craig woke up on November 4, 2016, with some sobering questions: How did it happen that our country has become so fractured and intolerant of opinions that don't align with our own? What can be done about it? Make Shift Coffee House was his answer. He has gone on to produce over 50 of these events, and he was given the American Award for Civic Collaboration for Community Innovation[4] in 2019.

I asked Craig what precisely he listens for in facilitating these events. "Well, right at the start of a coffee house, I'm listening for something that's going to be entertaining – I have to hook my audience! I'll ask 'Can you tell me more about that?' I'm looking for something passionate and honest in their response."

When I went through a MSCH training that Craig offered at the beginning of 2020, I asked him what he considered the biggest challenges in pulling together an event of this kind. His answer? "Getting conservatives to participate." He went on to say, "They are convinced that they are going to be attacked for their views."

This fear response to others who hold different political beliefs is an all-too-common reaction across the political spectrum, and it explains much of our current cultural climate. So how does Craig tackle this problem within a MSCH?

"I'll say something like, 'We've heard three points of view that all kind of seem like they're at the same end of the spectrum – I'd welcome a different opinion. 'When a difference of opinion is expressed, I support that person with my body language, with facial expressions, and with validation . . . extra attention. I'm trying to encourage other minority perspectives to speak up."

An article titled "Hard-Wired: The Brain's Circuitry for Political Belief"[5] based on a study by Emily Gersema and published in *Science News* describes an experiment with 40 participants who consider themselves progressive. They were given MRI scans to study brain reaction when exposed to statements challenging their political beliefs. The study found that people who were most resistant to changing their beliefs had more activity in the amygdalae and the insular cortex compared with people who were more willing to change their minds.

"The activity in these areas, which are important for emotion and decision-making, may relate to how we feel when we encounter evidence against our beliefs," said Jonas T. Kaplan, co-director of the Dornsife Cognitive Neuroimaging Center at USC and author of the article referencing the study. According to Kaplan, whenever we feel threat or anxiety, our insular cortex goes to work to process our physical sensations and will determine the emotional importance of the trigger. Understanding the interplay between the amygdala and the insular cortex supports the idea that when we feel threatened in some way, whether physically or emotionally, it's very difficult to change our minds.

Some of the responses described in similar experiments with college students also have to do with their expressed fear that exposure to different points of view will weaken the strength of their own convictions.

How does one maintain genuine curiosity against our internal amygdala-driven response?

Very few of us can actually accomplish this effectively on our own. It does not help when our culture considers those who soften their views or change their minds "spineless flip-floppers" or even "lacking in conviction".

Craig keeps his equilibrium by intensifying his curiosity less around what supports and proves a person's opinion (Head listening) and more by digging up the story of that person's experience informing the opinion (Heart listening). When we hear a true story, we have an emotional response, often an empathetic one, and we begin to build a bridge across difference from there.

But too much curiosity can also be a trap. "I have to pay attention to logistics," Craig tells me. "If we're two minutes away from adjournment, I can't lead this person into a long story, and I gotta be careful not to make too much of something if it's of particular interest only to me!"

If all goes well at a MSCH event, the person with a minority opinion who feels their story was truly heard most often will begin to trust the experience just a little more, and they may even come back for another one.

Craig articulates his hope that, through Make Shift Coffee House:

People have a new attitude towards those they disagree with. Attitude change translates into behavior change – where the person is more willing to strike up a conversation with somebody different, more willing to compromise with someone different and not dig in their heels. Ultimately, I hope it translates into policy making – how we make decisions in policy on our town councils, in state legislatures.

Craig's intentionality and creativity in producing Make Shift Coffee House as a tool for creating empathy between opposing sides is an effort specifically directed to help solve an entrenched cultural issue. This positions him squarely as a Hands listener.

## Empathy as Strategy for Winning the Argument

In a related vein, I listened to an interview recently with Bo Seo, author of a new book on debate skills titled *Good Arguments*.[6] Something he said resonated strongly with the need for deeper listening skills. As his family had immigrated from Korea to Australia when he was very young, Seo struggled to "get out of the shadows", to be seen and heard. He became intrigued by his school's debate program primarily because of the debate structure: timed intervals where only one person could speak and everyone else needed to really listen: not just "listen" until it was time for the speaker to stop, not just "listen" to poke holes in the opposing side's arguments, but listen, as Seo describes it, to actively utilize empathy.

Seo makes the distinction between empathy as it is considered in the debate world and the way empathy is considered in coaching and counseling. "Whereas most people viewed empathy as a spontaneous psychic connection, or a reflection of virtue, debaters knew it as an understanding achieved through a series of actions." Participants would methodically write down the other team's most salient points and actively incorporate them into their rebuttals, often by acknowledging the value of these elements. This strategy was also a way to literally "try on" another's perspective. Seo shares an activity called "Side Switch"[7] that exemplifies active empathy as a way to prep for a debate.

# Side Switch

Seo recommends this be done within five minutes of the start of a debate as a team warm up. Notice the active use of empathy as a strategy to sharpen one's own case.

He outlines three primary elements:

**Brainstorm:** First, all members of the team need to imagine they are on the opposing side. They are to brainstorm the four strongest points that support that opposing position and write these down on a clean sheet of paper.

**Stress-test:** Still in the opponent's mindset, they must now look over and review these arguments. What are the strongest possible objections to these points? Those objections are written in the margins of the paper.

**Loss ballot:** Now the team will need to mentally step into the winning shoes of the opposing side. They will write down the exact reasons why they won. They must also include any mistakes the opposite side may have made during the course of the debate.

The next steps will vary according to the specific situation and require the team to again take on their original perspective. The options from here are as follows:

They could revise one or two arguments in order to answer the possible objections they've discovered through taking the opponent's side.

They could revise any planned rebuttals against the arguments now expected from the other side.

They could devise roadblocks to thwart the other side's paths to victory.

I don't expect that anyone reading this book would be using it as a way to prepare for a debate, but Seo's premise in Side Switch is an example of the impact one can have in high-stakes interactions if one can "Set aside the certainty of one's convictions and see things from another point of view." We will explore this concept further utilizing a different tool in the upcoming "You Might Try This" section.

# The Coach's Perspective: Questions and Applications

1. If your coaching practice involves creating dialogue between feuding clients, how can you encourage the kinds of Hands listening demonstrated in Craig's story? In the Side Switch example?
2. Dismantling negative assumptions is so often a part of coaching and counseling clients through personal and professional disputes. How might you encourage clients to loosen the grip of these assumptions so that they can listen more proactively and communicate more clearly?
3. In some ways, the act of "labelling" others is really a refusal to listen more deeply to someone's story. How are your clients impacted by the labels others have given them? How are their relationships impacted by the labels they give others?

# You Might Try This . . . The Label Do-Over Project

This project was inspired by another intervention called the "Button Project" – where people are encouraged to make an actual button out of anything they choose that reflects the irritations that push their buttons. It was a lighthearted way to honor what irritates us, as well as poking a bit of fun at ourselves.

Years ago, I was asked to do a workshop for a non-profit focused on housing the homeless. Several surveys done over an 18-month span of time indicated that there were multiple issues and ongoing disputes within the ranks of those staff members who regularly engaged with the public. Decision makers in this organization discovered that recently hired staff who had been formerly homeless felt they were being subtly and not so subtly disrespected by the more seasoned staff. I was asked to create a workshop with this group of 20 to encourage trust and deeper listening. We heard many intense stories told by all the participants in these sessions. We reflected back on what we heard using some written material as well as some Playback structures and other techniques of reflective listening. In the next to the last session, the subject of labels and labelling came up in one of the debrief sessions. It was clear that there was lots of energy around this topic, so I created the Label Do-Over Project as a way to let go of labels we don't like and invent those we feel suit us better.

# Label Do-Over Project Instructions

Bring in any art supplies that you prefer – I provided glue, scissors, multi-colored Sharpies, a red magic marker for each participant, construction paper, pipe cleaners, and a pile of magazines for pulling images. Make sure you bring in enough materials for everyone to feel they have enough to use and choose from, but not so much that they feel overwhelmed by choices.

It is very important, particularly if you have multiple participants from different perspectives in the room, that they sit in mixed groups for this project.

The first label participants will create is the one they want to let go of. For example, those who had experienced homelessness used images that resonated with words like "Lazy", "Dirty", "Useless", and "Unskilled". Conversely, those who had always been housed constructed their labels from words like "Greedy", "Selfish", "Clueless", "In a Bubble", and chose images that reflected these assumptions.

Once the labels are constructed, you can ask each person to stand, show their label, and briefly explain why these images were chosen. When our group did this, the noise and chaos of the construction period subsided. As the labels were shown and explained, the hurtful power of the words and imagery silenced the group. It was as if time had completely stopped.

After the last label was shown, I instructed each participant to draw a large red "X" through their label, rip it into pieces, and step into the participant circle surrounding a trash receptacle. One by one, they are then asked to throw the pieces of the label into the trash. You could intensify this ritual by having them say something like "No more", "This label is no longer mine", or something to that effect. This continues until each person has thrown their label in the trash.

Now the construction of the desired label begins. I was surprised at the time, but I shouldn't have been, with how much people struggled with creating a label they wanted. Of course, it is easier to react and resent a label others place on us than it is to create a desired label of one's own. This is a process that asks people to envision themselves as something they may not yet have become. It asks them to be vulnerable and to share that vulnerability with the larger group.

I found it best to start small. I asked the participants to name some qualities in themselves that they were proud of: the group could then claim for themselves words like "resilient", "artistic", "empathic", "good listener". I encouraged them to add some more words and images to their label. The group continued with "Good strategist", "Team player", "Makes people laugh". The tone in the room shifted perceptibly to one of playfulness and possibility.

Again, once these new labels are completed, ask each participant to stand up and "claim" their new label by sharing what went into it. After each label, the room will applaud and cheer!

After the session debrief, I asked each participant to display this new label at their desks for awhile, as a reminder to themselves and others of their value in this particular work setting.

# Notes

1    Make Shift Coffee House: https://makeshiftcoffeehouse.com/
2    Good Group Decisions: https://goodgroupdecisions.com/
3    Deep Canvass: https://deepcanvass.org/

4    American Award for Civic Collaboration for Community Innovation: www. civvys.org/about

5    "Hardwired: The Brain's Circuitry for Political Belief", Kaplan, J.T., *Science News*, 2016

6    *Good Arguments*, by Seo, Bo, 2022

7    *Good Arguments*, Seo, page 176

# Tanya's Story: Going to the Dogs

For a number of years, I've been a member of a co-working space. Some time ago, the owner asked me to weigh in on a tricky issue that was percolating into a somewhat toxic brew. A few members, two or three of them, wanted to bring their dogs into the workspace. However, there were others who were very much opposed to this. The owner didn't want to come down hard on the dog proponents, but she was aware that those who did not want this change were feeling very unhappy. A few of the members had brought their dogs, with mixed results. At this point, it became clear our co-working community was on the verge of dividing into two camps with a calcifying binary, Dog Lovers vs. Dog Haters, and something needed to be done. I agreed to lead a conversation and also saw this as an opportunity to test out a new card game I had developed – Shift/POV[1] – for leading groups through conflicted conversations.

The most powerful moment of the meeting came when "Tanya" shared some insight as to why she did not want dogs in a workspace. "Every time one of the dogs barks here, at the mailman or whatever, alarms go off in my head and it takes about 20 minutes for me to get my focus back." she said softly. She then told us about roaming packs of feral dogs in the Asian city she was raised in. People would run for shelter when they heard the barking, and children who were too far from home often got bitten. "I've never gotten over that first response when I hear a dog bark. For me, it's pure panic".

The entire group was silent in listening to this story. No one rolled their eyes. No one minimized Tanya's experience with a trite label. The empathy we, as a group, discovered that day by listening to Tanya's story allowed us to move on and create a range of solutions. After a short

DOI: 10.4324/9781003296027-25

discussion, we reached a compromise amenable to all parties, and the topic has not come up again.

The group resolved the issue because we had taken the time to sort it out and listen to each other. We didn't just relay the "facts" of the situation, try to implement punitive rules, or come up with a quick Band-Aid fix. By listening with our hearts to that one simple, powerful story, we turned down the noise in the room, and in our world, just long enough to create solutions and strengthen the bonds of our community.

I checked in with Tanya later, and she admitted that she had been on the verge of pulling out of her membership completely over the dog issue. She was grateful the group meeting afforded her the space to be heard and was supportive of the amenable policy that resulted.

# The Coach's Perspective: Questions and Applications

1. How are your clients impacted by a rigid good-or-bad binary?
2. As coaches, part of our job is to elicit stories of authentic experience. What might happen if you encouraged your clients to get curious about the stories underlying negative experiences?
3. Particularly when there is strong emotional attachment, like the co-working members to their dogs, it can be difficult to encourage empathy to alternative points of view when clients are put on the defensive. How do you encourage curiosity as an antidote to hostile defensiveness?

# You Might Try This . . . Shift/POV

Note: The Shift/POV experience was designed as a card game for small groups, families, and working partners with a desire to process conflict and come to amicable consensus. It has also been used successfully in couples counseling. I include it here, as it requires strong listening skills in all the modalities, but particularly Heart and Hands listening.

Shift/POV (Point Of View) is an experiential learning structure for exploring difficult interpersonal dynamics in business teams, family groups, or public gatherings. I've designed this game as a way for participants to literally step into other points of view and to explore different angles of an issue they are trying to resolve. The experience takes place within three tightly timed discussion rounds intersected by the Random Factors – unique and surprising insight prompts that can encourage off the surface engagement, deeper listening, and curiosity.

A player's ability to set aside their own opinions and preconceived notions long enough to take in the opposing side's rationale is vital, particularly in the second discussion round.

I've divided the process into a series of steps with some questions for you, the coach and facilitator, to consider.

*Before You Start, Think About:*
- What one word would you choose to describe the communication in this group or couple?
- What quality do you believe would most benefit them in their interactions?
- What do you consider their top challenge in achieving that quality?

These answers will help you create the optimum experiential context in which to utilize the structure.

*Next: Take a Look at the POV Cards: Activator, Skeptic, and On the Fence*
The first discussion round of the three-round sequence is where participants make clear their authentic point of view regarding the issue. However, if you are working with a group that is strongly weighted to one side – six Activators to one Resistor, for example, feel free to assign POVs evenly for the first round, letting people know that they will have the opportunity to engage the issue from both opposing sides.

If you have a group smaller than six participants or are working with a pair of players trying to process a specific problem or dilemma, you'll want to eliminate the On-the-Fence position entirely.

If you have a group larger than ten, you may consider having On-the-Fencers assist you in noting interesting ideas and considerations in Rounds 1 & 2. Let them know that their input will be particularly valuable in Round 3. Essentially, the tool strives to get more people into the

On-the-Fence position, as this POV proves essential for developing comprehensive and collaborative solutions.

*Once You Have Chosen the POV Cards, You Can Select the Random Factors . . .*
The 45 Random Factor cards have been developed as insight and creativity prompts. Each suit: Actions, Questions, and Observations, is numbered so that the coach can strategically choose which cards would most benefit a particular group or couple and set the others aside.

Consider your answers to the questions on the previous page. My research has shown that problematic groups often fall into one of three general categories; Tentative, On the Surface, and Hyper-Competitive. The following general descriptions may serve as a guide.

*Tentative:*
Issues: Hesitant, polite, lack of trust, difficult to engage
Needs: Safe space for authenticity
Random Factor Cards 1–5 in all suits

*Stuck on the Surface:*
Issues: Impatient, rushed, distracted, "hates meetings", difficult to get their best input
Needs: Opportunities to slow down, become more mindful and "present" in the interactions
Random Factor Cards 6–10 in all suits

*Hyper-Competitive:*
Issues: Jostling for status, power over dynamics, lack of trust or mutual respect
Needs: To build focus on and appreciation for others, spark curiosity instead of judgment
Random Factor Cards 11–15 in all suits.

The Random Factors were developed to nudge participants out of their comfort zones and experience each other in different ways. They also provide you, the coach, with a means to strategically impact the emotional context the group will work within. It is advised that you choose at least 15 cards, but that is up to you. For smaller groups, you might also consider choosing one Random Factor card for each participant, placing them face down in front of each table position, and having the group change seats after each round. Shift/POV encourages you to come up with your own way of using the Random Factors – have some fun!

*How Shift/POV Is Played:*
Participants are asked to begin the first discussion round by picking a POV card: Activator, On the Fence, or Skeptic, relative to the issue being discussed.

From there, a participant's input into the first discussion will be determined by the card chosen. For example: An Activator could be aligned and enthused about a new idea or development; a partner or spouse might feel very strongly in favor of a particular action. A Skeptic would resist, and On the Fence will be encouraged to choose the side they are leaning towards as a way to experience full commitment to one point of view. Often, players will choose On the Fence because it is a "safe" position to take and does not conflict with either the Activators or the Skeptics. But if you are working with a group larger than 12 people, and the other two sides are amply represented, then those on the fence can be invited to deeply listen for both merits and holes in each opposing side, and you might call on them to report their observations after the discussion round ends.

The discussion proceeds for 7–10 minutes, any On-The-Fence observations are heard, and then everyone chooses a card from the Random Factor pile. Again, there are three kinds of cards here: Actions, Observations, and Questions. Participants will perform the activity, consider the question, or make the observation for a period of 1 minute, and then Round 2 of the discussion begins.

In Round 2, everyone engages the issue from the POV *opposite* their own starting position; for example, an Activator in Round 1 is now a Skeptic for Round 2, and vice versa. So Round 2 consists of Activators and Skeptics. Again, the action is timed for 7–10 minutes, and another Random Factor card is pulled. If a player paid only minimal attention to the other side's argument, then it will be embarrassingly obvious in the second round. As the facilitator of this process, you can decide whether you want to alert the group at the beginning of the experience to the listening requirements in Round 2 or let them discover that for themselves in the second round.

The third round is determined by where the group wants to go: either to tackle an issue that has come up in the first two rounds or begin brainstorming on possible ways forward, or there could be another option that presents itself. . . . It is not necessary to pick a POV card for the third round.

*Shift/POV Can Be Used as:*

- An initial warm-up activity prior to in-depth discussion, as it helps flesh out details and ramifications in the opposing sides and also encourages those On the Fence to better align with one or the other side or to articulate a third, "both-and" option.
- A means of encouraging authentic, deeper participation in exploring a well-defined issue.
- A pre-cursor to brainstorming, as everyone has a chance to articulate differing POVs and experience themselves and each other in taking risks and engaging the Random Factors.

# Note

1    Shift/POV, Dakin-Neal, Kym: https://kymdakin.com/shift-p-o-v/

# Hands Listening Heads Up . . . the Con Artist

I have to note here that there is a dark side to the Hands modality – con artists are particularly effective Hands listeners: they have a detailed grasp of the facts informing a victim's situation, along with (appearing to have) the Heart skills required to build trust, focused by the monetary motivation to take creative action on all that information.

I wondered how I might exemplify this issue of the Hands listening con artist in a way that would be relevant to coaching, when, to my knowledge, I've never coached one. And thankfully, I've not been the victim of this kind of crime.

Then I got curious about the psychological manipulation that destroys partnerships and marriages and whether there might be crossover with the listening strategies employed in creating a Ponzi scheme. I remembered a particularly notorious crime that came to light in the late 2000s. This has gone down in history as the most far-reaching and successful Ponzi scheme ever perpetrated in the United States. The con man's name was Bernie Madoff.[1]

In the early 1990s, electronic trading in the stock market was in its infancy, just waiting for someone to make their mark by applying artificial intelligence – such as it was then – as a means to accelerate order flow and mine in-depth market insights. Bernie Madoff was that someone.

He also had a chip on his shoulder. For decades, Madoff had run a very small investment firm that had to make money by "taking the crumbs", in his words, meaning to service the trades of small and micro investors that would be ignored by larger firms. Suddenly, as a result of his work in electronic trading, big banks were coming to him. He was finally part of the Wall Street "in crowd". He had skills, motivation, and now a

DOI: 10.4324/9781003296027-26

reputation. He would go on to become chair of the Nasdaq in 1990. He served in that capacity in 1991 and 1993 as well.

Madoff understood that the entire financial system is built on trust. The ability to gain trust is key to luring and retaining clients and essential in enhancing one's own reputation.

Trust, and the role of Head and Heart listening in establishing it, has been covered in previous sections. Hands listening combines the facts and data of Head listening, with the emotional attunement underlying Heart listening so that issues can be addressed and solutions developed. However, once established, a certain moral compass is required in order not to abuse the privilege of trust.

Many of us have known, or at least heard of, coaches who have made inappropriate use of the information and emotional vulnerability clients have entrusted to them. A coach is in a powerful position compared to a client seeking help. And if the needs of the coach rather than the client become the force that steers the relationship, if the Hands listening skills so key in helping solve client problems are turned toward purely benefiting the coach, then trouble is afoot.

In the heady, free-wheeling days of the 1990s stock market, a certain "sky's the limit" fever was building. Tech stocks had shown real promise, and people had money to invest, so the context that surrounded a player with a chip on his shoulder made playing fast and loose with other people's money very tempting.

Madoff understood his clients' need for financial safety: he successfully created a facade of respectability: his returns were high but not unreasonable, and he could claim to use a tried and true strategy: that of "collaring", also known as a split-strike conversion.[2] Collaring is utilized to minimize investment risk while protecting the original underlying shares.

Madoff also endeavored to build a facade of morality around his business by making charitable donations to organizations dear to the kinds of high-profile investors he wanted to attract. In this way, he was able to take advantage of a psychological vulnerability in human beings: we want to believe that someone who is altruistic cannot possibly be untrustworthy. And because investors came to trust Madoff as a person, they had a hard time believing that their investments were not sound. This is another vulnerability in the human psyche known as the "halo effect".[3]

Because he had developed not only the facts and data listening capacity he needed as a wall street financier but the Heart listening capacity to tune in to "the Dream" his clients were trying to build, he was able to perpetrate his scheme to defraud investors out of tens of billions of dollars. In 2009, he was sentenced to 150 years in prison, and he died there in 2021.

Hands listening can be a powerful and dynamic tool in creating change. Once you are familiar with this model, you can easily spot those with Hands listening as a primary modality. They are energetic, focused, and highly engaging. They appear to be gifted with the ability to take new information and synthesize it efficiently and effectively toward desired ends. Without sincere Heart listening however, as we have just seen in the Madoff story, it is also a skilled listening style that can wreak havoc.

## Hands Listening Modality Review: Section Summary

*As a review of the Hands listening modality, let's revisit these aspects:*

*Hand Listeners Listen for:*
- Problems to solve
- Actions to take
- A strategy
- New possibilities
- The future

*Hands Listeners Are Curious About . . .*
- What hasn't been tried yet?
- What else might work?
- Work-arounds
- The "how" in solving a problem

## The Strengths and Challenges of Hands Listening

*Hands listening provides:*
Connections between ideas for new applications

Connections that build bridges between difference
Multiple ways to consider a problem or issue
The ability to stay curious and follow internal promptings
A healthy relationship with risk
Adaptability, flexibility, and the capacity to change direction when necessary.

*Hands Listeners are challenged to:*
Manage time
Manage distractions
Prioritize activities that are associated with a singular goal
Persevere through obstacles and difficulty

*Hands listener professions and industries (not a complete list)*

| | | | | | |
|---|---|---|---|---|---|
| Recruitment | Lawyer | Start-ups | Journalism | Real estate | Graphic design |
| Travel | Sales | Lobbyist | Medical and legal advocacy | | Experiential learning |
| Architecture | Landscaping | Entrepreneurial development | | Animal training | |
| Sports training | Tech design | Interior design | Event planning | Renewable energy | |

# Positive Intelligence Crossover With Hands Listening

## *Saboteurs*

**Hyper Achiever:** Dependent on constant performance and achievement for validation and self respect. Latest achievement quickly discounted.

**Restless:** Constantly in search of greater excitement in the next activity or constant busyness. Rarely at peace or content with current activity.

## *Sage Powers*

**Innovate:** Curiosity and exploration in creating new ideas and solutions pertaining to specific problems.

**Activate:** The ability to take clear, focused action.

## *Balance and Amplify*

If you recognize yourself somewhere in this chapter, you may have strong Hands listening tendencies. You may also recognize the flip side of this modality when operating in a time-frame faster than others around you. Slowing oneself down in order to really be present to listen effectively is a challenge. I would offer an experiment to try:

- When someone is speaking to you, set yourself the task of asking at certain junctures: "Tell me more about . . ." and see if this might both slow you down and focus your attention off the surface of the exchange. Become aware as well of how this question affects your speaking partner.
- In your next conversation, challenge yourself to apply some "mirroring". The act of tuning in to the communication patterns: vocalics, gestures, and so on will encourage you to pay attention on a deeper level and make your partner feel more satisfied in the exchange.

If you find you would like to amplify some of the better Hands listening attributes, such as curiosity and creativity, try this:

Going into a conversation, get very clear about why you are listening and what you are listening for. Are you attempting to clear up confusion? Are you looking to dig deeper into certain elements of a topic? Are you looking to deepen a relationship? Getting clear about your goals will help you focus your questions according to desired outcomes. Additionally, you could better serve the conversation as a whole if you get clear about your partner's needs. Are they looking for information? An emotional connection? A straightforward critique? Don't be afraid to ask upfront. Most people appreciate the chance to clarify what they are after.

Are you a fan of lists? I find that oftentimes, making a list can help ease me through transitions of many kinds. Try making some fun yet challenging lists to encourage creativity and opening to new possibilities. If you give yourself permission to just put any old idea down under topics like: "10 Blogpost Titles on the Topic of Tap Dancing", or "20 Ways to

Get Out of Mowing the Lawn", you'll surprise yourself with how many workable ideas you can come up with. For more on this topic, check out a book titled *Become an Idea Machine* by Claudia Azula Altucher.[4] It's essentially a collection of prompts for creating ideas for specific uses. You can come up with your own lists based on activities you enjoy or are curious about and see how you feel after starting a few days with this action.

**Probing Questions . . .** Hands listeners may very much enjoy many of these questions and also struggle to answer some of them. It's all good information!

1. How did you choose your profession?
2. How has it changed you?
3. What are you most curious about?
4. At the end of your life, what will you look back on that most mattered?
5. What distracts you?
6. How do you keep yourself on task?
7. What makes you feel successful?
8. How does it feel to you to be vulnerable?
9. What feels most risky to you right now? How do you feel about that risk?
10. What makes a meaningful day for you?
11. What do you like to do outside of work?
12. What brings you joy?
13. What do you feel is your best contribution to those around you?
14. What frustrates you the most when people communicate with you?
15. What's your preferred form of communication?
16. What are your favorite metaphors?
17. What challenges are you faced with right now?
18. What makes a good day for you?
19. How do you make an unfamiliar place familiar to you?
20. What have you recently discovered or learned that surprised you?
21. What are you most certain about?
22. What do you do that lets you lose track of time?
23. What helps you learn/retain information the best?
24. Who/what has the most impact on you right now?
25. Please describe your optimum working environment

# Further Thoughts

Effective Hands listening can be considered the result of Head and Heart skills combined with the motivation to take action in a specific direction. Hands listeners are innate problem solvers but are prone to impatience and surface listening if the Heart modality is not strongly present.

As I further my research, I'm also intrigued by the possibility that Hands listening, all the modalities, actually, come in to play in what we consider serendipity. In Ruthie's story, I referenced *The Serendipity Mindset*, by Christian Busch. The author's premise illuminates the possibility that we can create our own luck by slowing down and paying attention to the potential connections between seemingly random occurrences.

The notion of connection between random elements also brings to my mind an effort I came across years ago called analogous field thinking, which is essentially the intentional meeting of vastly different areas of expertise and skillsets to solve problems. The effort was applied in a sampling of businesses in order to avoid the dreaded "Silo syndrome" so common in large companies. I just bet that there were several Hands listeners involved in coming up with this application!

By now, you most likely have a good idea about your own primary listening style, as well as that of some of your clients. Just in time, you are about to find out more about your particular listening skills in the next chapter!

# Notes

1    About Bernie Madoff: www.nasaa.org/4303/madoff-a-21st-century-ponzi-scheme/
2    Split Strike Conversion or "Collaring": www.risk.net/derivatives/1518427/madoff-fraud-puts-focus-due-diligence
3    Halo Effect: www.verywellmind.com/what-is-the-halo-effect-2795906
4    *Become an Idea Machine*, Azula Altucher, Claudia, 2015

# PART 5

# Listening Inside and Out

# 23 | Discover Your Listening Modalities: The Assessments

As you've been reading through the previous chapters, you may have a sense of what your listening modalities may be, and you may have already begun to notice and experiment. That's my hope. But if not, I invite you to participate in a short assessment to get a bit closer to identifying your modalities.

You can go about this in two ways: You can fill out the assessment on paper by answering the questions that follow. And/or – you can listen to the story I'll tell you via a YouTube video. Find my YouTube channel under Kymberly Dakin, and then access the Listening Style Assessment Story[1] from there. I pause at certain junctures in this three-part story to give you time to log what you've retained. Then I'll move on to the next part of the story, and you'll again write down what you remember. Once you've completed your third section notes, you can score your assessment at the end of this chapter.

Following, you'll find 12 questions and possible responses to the Listening Modalities Assessment. I think you'll find this pretty straightforward in method but surprising in your results. After each of the three possible responses, gauge your likely reaction to all three possibilities according to this scale:

**1. Less Likely 2. Somewhat Likely 3. Highly Likely**

For example, for question 1, your response might look like:

- Continue to be intrigued by the specifics of what he is relaying? 3
- Be impatient and feel as if you've lost the point of the conversation? 1
- Be distracted by his frequent gestures and changes in vocal tone? 2

DOI: 10.4324/9781003296027-28

# It's Very Important to Gauge All Three Responses!

After you've answered all 12 questions, you'll be given instructions for final tallying. I know I don't have to remind you to be as honest as possible with your responses, but do have some fun, too!

# The Modalities Assessment

Welcome to the Listening Modalities Assessment! After each of the three possible responses, gauge your likely reaction to all three possibilities according to this scale:

### 1. Less Likely   2. Somewhat Likely   3. Highly Likely

1.  **You and a new member of your work team are meeting for the first time. It's clear his information is very granular and quite comprehensive. After 10 minutes of listening to him nonstop, how likely are you to:**
    A. Continue to be intrigued by the specifics of what he is relaying?
    B. Be impatient and feel as if you've lost the point of the conversation?
    C. Be distracted by his frequent gestures and changes in vocal tone?
2.  **It's your fourth Zoom call at the end of the workday. There are eight others on the call. The facilitator begins to struggle with screen share. How likely are you to:**
    A.  Offer to help her by describing the steps to screen sharing?
    B.  Distract yourself by checking your email?
    C.  Be aware of her discomfort and let her know it's okay to move on?
3.  **You're in a very busy airport. You've just found out your flight is delayed by two hours. What are you likely to do *first*:**
    A.  Repeatedly check the airline's app for updates about your flight?
    B.  Call ahead to your destination to let them know your flight may be late?
    C.  Be distracted and captivated by the conversations of people around you?

4.  **You are in a work meeting. Your team is trying to make a decision. How likely are you to be distracted by the following factors when listening to someone else?**
    A.  Tech distractions: cellphone, emails, texts, and so on?
    B.  Time issues, your own impatience?
    C.  Other people's emotional tone, facial expression, and body language?

5.  **You are being interviewed for a job. How likely are you to consider the interview successful if it includes the following:**
    A.  Excellent exchange of information?
    B.  Clear next steps?
    C.  Animated dialogue?

6.  **How likely are these situations to *challenge* your ability to listen?**
    A.  Overhearing a highly animated and emotional exchange between colleagues?
    B.  A spouse repeatedly complaining about a parent over the last two months?
    C.  A two-hour lecture – on anything!?

7.  **Recall a politician you've heard recently. How likely are you to focus on:**
    A.  The detailed information the speaker imparted?
    B.  The topic's relevance to a particular problem of interest to you?
    C.  Messaging underneath the words: the speaker's frame of mind, tone of voice, body language, what *wasn't* spoken?

8.  **You are in the audience for a panel discussion with three panelists. The topic is one of great interest to you. How likely are you to pay attention to:**
    A.  Speaker 1 – a recognized authority in the field; her content is very data driven and granular, and she offers lots of substantiation for her premise?
    B.  Speaker 2 – a somewhat controversial figure in that he has come up with a new and yet to be proven angle on the topic?
    C.  Speaker 3 – a college student who recently won an award for the humanitarian application of work in this field. She is clearly nervous but very passionate about her subject?

9.  **You get a call from an important client. There is a problem with the product you sold him. He states "This application is not working with our computers. Everyone here is having the same issue and we've got several projects due this week!" How likely are you to focus on:**

A.  The information surrounding and leading up to the issue?

B.  Any clues as to how the problem can be addressed right now?

C.  The vocal and emotional tone of your client on this call?

10. **You are in the midst of an extremely stressed and busy day. Your sister calls you with concerns about your mother. "Mom is acting very strange. I went over to her house just now and she didn't recognize me at first. She forgot that she had asked me to bring her that book she wanted to borrow –** *The Aging Brain.* **Aging brain! I think she's got dementia!" How likely are the following factors to focus your attention.**

A.  Details like: "She didn't recognize me" "*The Aging Brain*" "She's got dementia!"

B.  The word "dementia"?

C.  The worried tone in her voice?

11. **You have agreed to coach a new client on an upcoming presentation as a favor to a colleague. All information to this point: fees, meeting times, minimum and maximum time commitment, have been relayed via email. When you meet the client however, it's clear the person speaks extremely softly and can't make eye contact with you. How likely are you to begin the session by** *first* **doing the following:**

A.  Get information on the client's background and history with presentation and public speaking?

B.  Speak to and address the client's obvious challenges in making effective presentations?

C.  Prioritize the client's comfort level by first asking some off-topic questions?

12. **You are going on a first date with someone a friend has set you up with. In conversation with this person for the first time, how likely are you to feel a positive connection to this person, based on:**

A.  How knowledgeable the person seems to be – the extent of their expertise and detailed knowledge of a topic of interest to you both?

B.  The level of focus and energy the person conveys – direct questions, surprising answers to your questions, degree of authenticity?

C.  How "tuned in" to you this person appears to be: they ask interesting questions, they have animated facial expressions, and there is a lot of "mirroring" going on?

## Scoring the Assessment

Tally your total scores for the first responses only in each scenario (the A questions), then the second (B questions) responses only, and then the C questions. The highest tally will reveal your primary listening modality, and the second highest total is your secondary listening modality. The third modality is one you most likely use the least.

Highest Score in the "A" responses: Primary Head Listener
Highest Score in the "B" Responses: Primary Hands Listener
Highest Score in the "C" Responses: Primary Heart Listener

## Note

1   Listening Style Assessment Story YouTube: www.youtube.com/watch?v=OZNKWphsBfA

# Conclusion: Listening in a Larger Sphere

## Group Think

Several years ago, I had the opportunity to do some work with a small governmental entity. I was invited to help a specific team of seven women with communication issues. The initial meeting with the team manager, "Claire", was cordial, polite, and positive, but I had a difficult time getting her to state what exactly the communications problem was that needed addressing. Every question I asked was met with an enthusiastic plug for how well the team was doing and the protocols the team had put in place for ease and consistency in sharing information, but no specific reason as to why they wanted someone outside their organization to do communications work. I finally asked her when I'd be able to meet with the entire team. My hope was that I could get my questions answered once I talked to them. We made arrangements to meet with the team the following week. She, however, made clear that she needed to be in the meeting as well. I got an unsettled feeling.

The meeting started out well. It was clear these women enjoyed working together, and there was a high degree of camaraderie. But once I turned the conversation from "getting to know you" to more concrete concerns as to what problems had arisen that required an outside communication consultant – the room fell silent.

Claire then offered, "We thought we'd like to get some new ideas for team building". Laura, Charlene, Joyce, and Tammy each nodded and expressed agreement, almost in unison. I could feel palpable relief spreading around the table.

"Well," I began, a bit hesitantly, "Team building is a rather general term, and I heard previously from you all that you feel you function well

174

DOI: 10.4324/9781003296027-29

as a team." Again, heads nodded around the table. I continued into what I felt was going to be trickier terrain. "If there are some specific reasons why you feel your group needs team building, or culture adjustment of some kind, or better communication strategies, that would give me a place to start building a program for you."

No one made eye contact with me. And "team building" was reinforced as the end result they hoped for. The meeting ended politely and cordially, but I never did get a direct response to my question. I eventually took a pass on providing this training.

Sometime later that month, I spoke to a colleague who was a good friend of one of the women on that team. Claire had been in her team manager position for about six months. While she was efficient and competent, she did not follow up on input, feedback, or suggestions made by the rest of the group, many of whom had decades of experience in the field. She would simply nod politely and then proceed the way she had wanted to go.

As a result, the team had decided it was easier to take a back seat and just go along to get along. They stopped sharing their opinions, ideas, and even new information that would counter the manager's assessment. And they even went further in the interests of keeping their employment. The group as whole tended to reinforce this passivity by discouraging their members from speaking truth to power. The "communications training" had been suggested by the department's superior, who must have sensed something amiss. In declining that contract, I felt like I had dodged a bullet.

The underlying issue on this team appeared to be not only the behaviors of a controlling manager who wasn't truly listening to her reports, but it was the decision by the rest of the group to simply stop trying to be heard. The result was diminished input, reduced trust on all sides, and lessened productivity overall.

Cass Sunstein and Reid Hastie, in their book *Wiser: Getting Beyond GroupThink to Make Groups Smarter*,[1] described a similar dynamic. "If you have information that is jarring or disruptive, and you speak out, your colleagues might look at you funny or like you a bit less."

The entire culture of the team I had encountered was caught in a restrictive social vise, much of it rooted in one individual's inability to listen to her team. As a result, she was robbed of their experience, their history and their creativity. Like a virus, a palpable shutdown had taken hold and had become self-reinforcing. Even though the team may have kept their jobs, everyone ultimately loses in this kind of situation.

By contrast, this next story will highlight a very different kind of leader.

# Leaders Who Listen

I was a 20-something professional actor wannabe in New York City. Between some small exciting successes, bills had to be paid, so money had to be made. Temping at several employment agencies was how I made it. One of my longer-term assignments was assisting an investment manager, "Gregory", in a large corporate bank on Wall Street.

My working attitude at that time was not unusual for a 20-year-old with her sights set on fame and glory. I would simply do the temp job I was hired for, but I would invest no more focus, time, or energy than the absolute minimum required to get my paycheck and pay those bills. (This may sound like the recent "Quiet Quitting" attitude embraced by many workers post-pandemic.) I was cordial and professional, and my authenticity was absolutely shuttered from 9–5, Monday through Friday.

This attitude had gotten me through many a temporary job, and though I was offered permanent employment at a number of places, I also had a front row seat to what was required of full-time employees. Many of them put in upwards of 60 hours a week, working at the behest of men (and in the late 80s and early 90s, they were overwhelmingly men) who would routinely growl at colleagues, bark at staff, and of course ignore lowly temps. They were stressed, overbearing, often overweight, and simply toxic. Aside from the money, I couldn't fathom the appeal of working in a culture like this. I would come in on time, leave promptly at 5 PM, often without saying anything to anyone, and practically run out the door.

One Friday, while working for Gregory, something shifted. He called me into his office on my return from lunch and asked me to sit down. In my mind, I started rifling through the various projects he had assigned me, thinking I must have done something very wrong, as our exchanges in the three weeks I'd worked for him were pretty perfunctory.

He hunched over his desk and gestured to the piles of paperwork that covered every surface in his office, and exclaimed "I hate all of this". He shook his head and sighed. Then he looked at me and smiled ruefully, "And I can only imagine how you must feel." My mouth . . . may have dropped open.

He then asked me "What would it take for you to become a little more committed to the work you do here?"

I didn't know how to answer. I honestly had never thought about it. And it's a question no one had ever asked me. "Uhm . . . I'm not sure I know what you mean . . . ?" may have been all I managed.

He nodded. "Well, I'd like you to think about it over the weekend, and come back with some ways we could make this job more appealing to you." He gestured again at the piles on his desk. "It's obvious that it's going to take a lot of work to clean this mess out, and I can't do it alone. I need your focus and commitment. You do everything I ask you to do correctly and on time, but I need you to take more initiative, so I don't always have to be giving you instructions. I know this job is not what you want to do with your life. So I'm asking what we can do to make the rest of your time here better for you, so that you can commit more of yourself to it, while you're here."

You could have knocked me over with a feather.

Let's take a look at what happened in that exchange.

First, in starting off our interaction with the statement "I hate all of this" Gregory revealed some transparency and personal vulnerability. I instantly saw him as a human being – not a corporate cog in the wheel. His next statement "I can only imagine how you must feel" indicated that he saw my situation with a degree of empathy. He couldn't have gotten my attention more effectively. Then he asked for my input. He offered to make changes in my working situation that would better serve me – the lowly temp – and he asked me to come up with them.

I did think about possible changes in my work situation that weekend. On Monday morning, I came in with a few that I was sure would get eye rolls. I walked into Greg's office. He was on the phone, so I went to leave, but he gestured for me to sit down. He told the person on the phone that he had an appointment, he concluded that call, and he turned his full attention on me.

After the usual morning greetings and the "how was your weekend" routine, he got right to it. "What did you come up with for changes?"

I swallowed. But this is what he'd asked for. I took a deep breath.

"Physical space is important to me." I began. I watched him nod, his eyes directly on mine, his posture open and available. I continued. "Gray cubicles depress me. They make me feel like I need to take a nap." This made him laugh, and then he offered, "I can relate to that!"

Okay, I thought, here goes. "I would like to be moved, if possible (and I totally thought it wasn't) to one of the cubicles on the opposite side of the floor – where the windows are."

He looked thoughtful. "I think that can be arranged."

"And I'd like to bring some stuff from home to kind of create better surroundings in that space. More color. Nice photos, maybe a painting. Stuff like that."

He nodded. "No problem."

I prefaced the next request with a question: "Gregory, I notice you are always here earlier than me. What time do you usually arrive?"

He tilted his head at my question and leaned back in his chair. A slight smile crossed his face. "7:30 or 8."

I swallowed. "Well, there's a class I'd like to take a couple days a week, but it starts right at 5 PM. If I came in at 8:30 on those days, could I leave at 4:30 so I can get on the subway in time to make the class?"

He shrugged and said, "I don't see why not." Then he thought for a moment. "But here's the thing." He gave me that direct look again. "I need for you to let me know ahead of time what days you'll be leaving early, and you'll have to remind me on those days." I nodded. "And." He shifted in his seat and clasped his hands on the desk, leaning toward me. "Each evening, before you leave, you'll need to come in and say goodbye, okay?"

"Deal." I said.

This simple exchange completely transformed our working relationship from then on. Once I got the changes I had asked for in time and space, working there became physically more pleasant, but more than that, Gregory had listened to me with empathy and problem-solving intentionality, and he continued to do this as time went on. I found my commitment to helping him deepened exponentially as we continued to work together. When my tenure there ended, I was even a bit sorry to be leaving, and Gregory said he was sorry to see me go.

Leaders who can effectively employ Head, Heart, and Hands listening build organizations able to:

- Adapt to ongoing change
- Encourage transparency

- Actively engage and utilize employee input across multiple levels
- Build trust within their workplace as well as with their global partners
- Inspire high degrees of creativity and employee loyalty
- Enjoy productive, respected relationships with surrounding communities

All that sounds great, but leaders like Gregory are still pretty rare. How can we coach leaders to more effectively listen in such a way that these benefits can be achieved?

For some time now, our cultural model of leadership has been very consistent. Leaders are "born to lead". They are charismatic, visionary individuals driven to succeed in a high-stakes, volatile business climate. They may be difficult to work with, and their companies may experience high rates of staff turnover (particularly post-pandemic) as a result of their leadership style, but stakeholders and corporate boards continue to applaud them as long as the stock price stays high. As coaches, however, we have witnessed the effect of this relentless pace on these driven individuals, their families, and the culture of the companies they have built. And it can be costly.

As a practicing coach, perhaps you have, or strive to have, some of these "born leaders" as clients. As you listen to them in your sessions, you might begin to notice what they pay attention to – what they are actively listening for as well as what they misheard or did not hear at all. They may not understand the underlying issues that have made life so difficult for them, so it becomes your job to get them listening for different information.

As you no doubt know by now, the concept of required leadership traits is evolving. I was curious about exactly how, so I dug into several sources – *Harvard Business Review*, *Asana*, and *Forbes* among them. The list that follows here from Northeastern University[2] is an accurate compilation of what I discovered.

# Five Qualities of Effective Leaders

1. **They are self aware and prioritize personal development:** They know how to listen to their own authenticity as well as their inner compass; they encourage the same in others.

2. **They focus on developing the careers and capacity of others:** Leaders who seek to inspire those around them to be all they can be need first to inspire trust. Trust is built from listening with empathy, thereby creating safe space for authenticity. Career development can then grow from a solid foundation.

3. **They encourage strategic thinking, innovation and action:** Leaders who can guide and inspire, *without controlling the outcome*, and who can apply effective Hands listening often achieve higher rates of innovation and creativity in their organizations.

4. **They are ethical and civic minded:** Leaders who demonstrably "walk their talk" command trust and respect from those around them and provide ballast in times of stress, uncertainty, and unforeseen change. They intentionally widen their perspective to include the community impacted by their organization and make concerted efforts to make sure their business is perceived as a value-added community player.

5. **They practice effective cross-cultural communication:** Difference sparks curiosity, not fear, in effective leadership, especially when dealing with needed change. Leaders who convey respect and appreciation for the efforts of those from different cultures *and insist on accountability for those who convey the opposite* set a tone of cultural inclusion.

If you work in an organization with these principles activated, then you most likely have someone at the helm who is intentional in creating this kind of culture. My encounter with Gregory was a small example of this kind of intentionality. If you run an organization of any kind, you can be sure that your employees will give you their utmost best when they feel listened to, trusted, and engaged. Part of the challenge, as we have seen and experienced, is making intentional listening a priority and supporting the value of better listening to enhance our personal and professional lives.

Can you imagine our world with leaders at the helm who know how to listen with empathy and build bridges between difference? Who can inspire others through compassionate example? As coaches, we can help build this capability in our clients. In fact, given the state of our world right now, this work has never been more important.

# Listening for Community Healing: Restorative Justice

Some of us may remember a powerful film that came out in 2008 titled *Flowers of Rwanda – Making Peace with Genocide*.[3] At the heart of the movie lies the question: Can a country heal after experiencing a horrific genocide that claimed the lives of over 800,000 people? An answer provided by the film is a way forward through the applied principles of restorative justice.

This method of communal healing came to the notice of the world through South Africa's Truth and Reconciliation Commission (TRC)[4] after the end of Apartheid in 1994. Authorized by Nelson Mandela and chaired by Desmond Tutu, the TRC was intended to create a forum where South African citizens could witness the stories of victims, perpetrators, and impacted others. It was designed to create an official record of human rights violations and to provide opportunities for offenders to offer reparation to victims, as well as for victims to offer forgiveness. The commission also established a register of reconciliation so that ordinary South Africans could express regret and remorse for their own past failures and offenses.

In the writing of this book, I became interested in how a process such as restorative justice (RJ) might impact the listening of those who take part in it. Our current justice system is focused primarily on finding the true perpetrator of a crime and meting out the appropriate punishment. The offender then lives the rest of their lives under the label of "criminal", even after release.

It's a system that demands a rigid "defense versus prosecution" lens and operates within its own very clear right-and-wrong, black-and-white binary. Punishment of the offender is then supposed to make the victim feel that their injury has been redressed. But in too many instances, this is felt not to be the case.

Before we move on, however, I must clarify that my exploration of this model is made with the intention to analyze the listening skills used in a restorative justice experience and how they may differ when compared to our current criminal justice model. It is not my intention to comment on the integration of restorative practices or to advocate for the replacement of our current justice system.

I spoke with Dr. Joe Lasley, PhD, assistant professor of leadership and organizational studies[5] at the University of Southern Maine and board member on the Restorative Justice Institute of Maine,[6] to get his insights on RJ applications.

Dr. Lasley uses the principles of RJ as a tool in his consulting practice, focused on leadership and building more meaningful community experience. Restorative justice procedures (he called them circle facilitation and restorative conversations) are one of many tools he puts forward to advance in-depth communication and learning.

In our interview, Dr. Lasley was very clear about the contrast between an RJ process and the standard criminal justice system at work in our country at present.

> In our system, if you commit a crime, you get labeled a criminal and you are punished, and then you're stuck. In restorative justice, the crime doesn't get erased or washed away, but you move forward. You go through the process of actually repairing and apologizing, and then you rejoin the community as a full member again, not as a black sheep.
>
> The deeper magic of restorative practice is the healing power of forgiveness, particularly for those who forgive others, even more than for those who are forgiven. This is where the deepest kind of listening occurs.

I'd like to illustrate this difference and discern the listening modalities involved by using a hypothetical example.

A robbery of a small bakery takes place in a neighborhood within a large city. The bakery has been a community fixture for decades. It is owned and staffed by one large, multigenerational family.

On a Friday night in late June, the bakery is robbed by a young man, his face covered with a mask. The manager, Lois, a woman in her 50s, tries to prevent him from taking the week's proceeds, and she is knocked unconscious for her efforts. After holding the other two workers at gunpoint and cleaning out the register, the thief flees the scene. The workers – Taylor and Sam, the manager's adult children – call an ambulance for their mother. Then they alert the police.

Within 24 hours, the police have arrested a young man from the same neighborhood after a witness identifies him. Lois has a sustained concussion. Doctors express doubt that she can return to her job any time soon.

Five months go by, and the young man (we'll call him William) is on trial for armed robbery. Lois, Taylor, Sam, and Harper, the man who identified William, are called as witnesses. The courtroom is filled with members of the community who are instructed to stay quiet while the trial is in session. William's mother, Valerie, sits supported by her other children. From time to time, she quietly weeps.

The stories of the victim and the accused are heard through very defined lenses. Others surrounding the offense are asked for their stories as witnesses to some aspect of the crime and questioned in a way that intentionally augments either the defense or the prosecution's case. Their input is limited to the provable facts of what took place on that evening in June.

The ending to this story is one we are all familiar with: William is pronounced guilty as charged. He receives a jail sentence, and regardless of how long he serves, he will never be able to escape the cultural taint of those who have been incarcerated. His every move will be accompanied by suspicion. Any effort he makes to try and reclaim his life will be met with distrust. Lois may or may not completely heal from her physical injuries. She and her family will have to carry on as best they can. The bakery will survive, but now, certain young men in the neighborhood, some of them from a certain family, will be greeted not with the usual friendliness and banter but with a terse silence and transactional distance, at best. In this instance, the injury to the neighborhood culture has been nowhere considered or addressed.

Alternatively, if the case had been explored within a restorative justice structure, and if the community had deemed RJ appropriate for this case, the outcomes may have been very different for everyone involved: victim, offender, witnesses . . . and community.

As I mentioned at the top of this section, restorative justice is appropriate only in cases where specific accountability criteria[7] have been met – primarily that the perpetrator is not a repeat offender and has expressed sincere and authentic regret. Law enforcement, community leaders, and impacted others are involved in making that determination.

When one is actively listening in order to build a bridge between disputing parties, when one intentionally tunes in to multilevel communication cues: facial, physical, and others, in order to discern the truth beneath the words and to heal the impact of an injustice, the listening modalities are different from those used in the western judicial system. The dispassionate Head listening lens is moved from primary to peripheral so that witnesses, circle leaders, and facilitators can encourage and intentionally utilize empathic Heart listening.

William's trial would then become more of a facilitated conversation between victim and offender so that each party would gain contextual clarity around the actions in question. William would hear about the costs of his action on the victim, her children, and her business. The conversation would extend to members of the neighborhood who now suffer the palpable negative effects of broken community trust.

Dr. Lasley believes that this community input is one of the most important aspects of restorative justice.

> Everyone who's in the circle is a full participant in a situation where someone has harmed another person, or committed an act that has harmed a group. If you're not the person who was harmed or did the act, you're still in the circle for a reason, whether you're a supporter or a community member or someone who simply cares about the people involved. And that is an important role, not a secondary role, because everyone is a full participant in the circle. So that is key to the whole process in the end.

In William's case, detailed stories are elicited, and the necessary time is taken for all to be heard. William's life situation and the context surrounding the crime are heard and understood but do not excuse his actions. Deciding exactly what reparations are required after having heard experiences from all sides is where the problem-solving skills of Hands listening are put into play. William has input into what he needs to do to redress this crime. He is asked by his surrounding community to make amends. And those affected by the crime can experience the gift of offering forgiveness. Dr. Lasley concludes,

> By listening deeply to the stories of the harm he has caused, William can take responsibility for working towards repair as part of his

community and with their support. This requires everyone involved to listen deeply, indeed it is community listening.

The intentionality in the listening depicted in this version of William's case resonates with the five Rs of Restorative Justice: Relationship, Respect, Responsibility, Repair, and finally Reintegration.

In the film *Jirga*[8] that I found a reference to in the book *The Upside of Uncertainty*,[9] the authors describe a dramatic instance of forgiveness. *Jirga* follows the story of an Australian soldier battling the Taliban who, in the midst of a village raid, kills an innocent man – the father of three children. Unable to assuage his feelings of guilt, the soldier returns to the village three years later to make amends and is put on trial. The eldest son, holding a knife to the throat of his father's killer, does not, in fact, slit his throat. The tribespeople then express the film's lesson: "Forgiveness is mightier and more honorable than taking revenge."

Where is there a process in our current western justice system that emphasizes forgiveness? It's a question worth asking, particularly now in these times of so much distrust and division.

Once I had done some research on the RJ process, I found myself curious as to whether the principles of RJ could be applied to situations not necessarily involving crimes and wrongdoing. Are there instances where RJ could benefit working culture? How about coaching clients going through divorce? Family disputes? Car accidents? For many of us, this would require a mental shift away from the purely punitive actions implied by "justice" and into the less familiar territory of "restorative". Again, Dr. Lasley provides experiential insights:

> One of the things that I appreciate the most about [restorative justice] is that it lends a structure for group process to really happen because it equalizes voices. I've used it as a staff development tool, and in team training. Circle practices are very useful for giving voice and getting participants to listen in ways that are different than our normal habits.
>
> So when you apply some of what you have learned in Restorative Justice to leadership, organizational development, circle participation, regular structures, and when you allow people to come together, they can talk about the impact that certain changes are having on

them. It can be a way for the group to deal with loss, for example, or if the group is going through a particularly impactful challenge. So you intentionally create conversations where people can share off the surface and deepen their connection to each other to literally create a working community.

"Listening in ways that are different from our normal habits", listening and sharing off the surface, requires a different, whole-body method of taking in information. Restorative justice exemplifies, in particular, the benefit of shifting Head listening to a secondary role in order to access the benefits of Heart and Hands listening.

Finally, I'll share some results from a study on the effectiveness of RJ titled "Are Restorative Justice Conferences Effective in Reducing Repeat Offending? Findings from a Campbell Systematic Review".[10]

After an exhaustive analysis of over 500 cases, the 10 that passed the rigorous inclusion criteria led researchers to the conclusion that Restorative Justice Conferences (RJCs) do cause a small but very cost-effective reduction in repeat offenses. The estimate for the British experiments conducted in both the United Kingdom and Canada found a ratio of 3.7–8.1 times more benefit in cost of crimes prevented than the cost of delivering the RJCs.

# Deep Canvassing – The Heart of Changing Minds

A dear friend and colleague of mine, Bill Dufris, created a huge sign and stuck it on his lawn when Donald Trump was president. In large letters, it asked the question "What Would Jesus Do?" It showed two illustrations. In the first, Trump is walking through water with Jesus following behind him. In the second, Jesus is shown dunking Trump into the water.

A neighbor Bill had not previously met showed up at his door one day: an elderly woman, nervous but resolute, and asked him to take down the sign. He invited her in to talk about it. No one was kinder or friendlier, easier to talk to than my late great friend Bill. But she pursed her lips, shook her head, and marched back down the porch stairs.

So here's my question – how might that conversation have taken place? What would Bill have had to do to make it safe enough for her to tell the story behind her demand?

Right as I was finishing this book, a friend introduced me to deep canvassing[11] If you are not familiar with it, you may find the term a bit off-putting. You may have associations, like I did initially, with the "Deep State", like Big Brother digging into your political opinions. But that is not at all the intent of this effort.

Wikipedia offers this definition: a form of political canvassing "that uses long empathic conversations to help shift someone's beliefs." And from the Deep Canvass Institute: "Deep canvassing is talking with strangers – about hopes, fears and aspirations. We reach across differences to build connections and trust through conversation." This is Heart listening intentionally applied to build bridges across difference.

The act of getting into a deep meaningful conversation with a stranger – one who holds beliefs antithetical to your own – has to start with deep listening. This is not easy. It asks us to set aside our own agenda and actively, intentionally seek resonance with a stranger in order to build empathy.

Why is it so difficult for many of us to have deep empathic conversations, especially when it's very clear how much we need to have them in our neighborhoods, our workplaces, our interpersonal relationships? I suspect they don't happen because we fear we will be exhausted by them. But what if, instead, we feel energized and inspired?

In every election cycle over the last eight years, I've volunteered to do phone canvassing to help get out the vote. Most of the time, I reach no one, as we are all annoyed by these calls and have ways of blocking them. Deep canvassing, however, holds much richer potential if I can find the time, the focus . . . the courage.

# The Listening Hour

Ten women sit outdoors in a circle. Each chair is carefully spaced six feet away from the next. There is a fire pit in the center, but the warmth of its flames cannot reach us through the icy rain.

We have gathered here to share our stories; listen deeply to those of our companions; and, for this brief time, counteract the isolation that afflicts us all to varying degrees.

When the world shut down due to Covid, the damage done to interpersonal communication was extensive and may impact multiple generations for years to come. However, this crisis has also birthed new forms of experience dedicated to connecting us deeply across distance and culture.

One of these efforts is titled the "Listening Hour".[12]

Launched in 2020 by Jonathan Fox,[13] also the founder of Playback Theatre,[14] the Listening Hour was created as a means of honoring story as our primary means of creating relationship, compassion, empathy, and understanding.

In our circle, "Liza" is speaking. She is in the chair to my right. I watch her snuggle deeper into her rain slicker as she begins her story, the raindrops dripping from her hood. "Jenny" asks her to speak up – it's hard to hear Liza's soft voice against the rain and the sounds of traffic on the other side of the house. She begins telling us about the dream she had last night. The dream was about her brother, her twin, who was stillborn. This is a dream she has had several times over the years, but since the pandemic, what she calls "this visitation" has increased in frequency.

In practice, these hours are facilitated, often on Zoom, via a Guide whose primary job is to create safe space for a small group to share stories. There are often no themes, no designated topics, and no expectation for any circle member to speak or to share, but there is a great deal of respectful listening going on. Participants will pick up a thread from one teller and share a story of their own, or they will simply offer an experience that has come up for them in that place and time.

When Liza finishes relaying her dream, we are all quiet. Our Guide – Amanda, invites us to breathe deeply and consider the images in Liza's story. She then invites whomever would like to speak next to share any reflections that Liza's sharing may have prompted. I feel deeply honored that Liza has shared this very personal story with us. I have known her for some time – around five years – and never knew her birth story or the dream that has haunted her for so much of her life.

Once those who wish to respond do so, Amanda invites the next story. Rachel volunteers, and she mentions that Liza's dream reminded her of a story that involves her brother and his struggles with substance abuse. We continue to listen. We continue to share, with silence, breathing, and reflection in between stories. Any impulse we may feel to "fix" or offer advice to anyone after they share is very gently but firmly muted. The whole point of the circle is to allow the power of storytelling and story listening to work its own particular magic.

All the while, Amanda stays quiet, simply listening, perhaps taking notes. But she intentionally looks for connections, repeated images, and possible themes in the stories told. She employs Head listening in remembering important facts, Heart listening to tune in to the emotions, Hands listening in finding commonalities and crossover. Once everyone who wishes to share has done so, Amanda verbally shares these "red threads" of connection that serve to reinforce and amplify the experience of the group. She may connect the red threads in a simple narrative, or she may weave them into a new story, one that belongs to all of us as we shiver around the circle. Despite the distance between us, despite the sleet, despite all that calls us away from the circle and back into our lives, we are brought closer to each other; we have deepened our connection to each other, simply through the act of deep listening.

I attended a few of these Listening Hours while our world was still in the grip of a raging pandemic. At first, I thought the process felt a bit like "therapy". It became clear, however, that the power of simply listening to stories *without being expected to say anything after* can feel a bit therapeutic. Having others listen to my story with the same amount of attention allowed me to feel deeply heard without being dependent on verbal response. The final "weaving" together of a singular story's images, themes, metaphors, and emotions helped us feel that we all had contributed to the story "soup". In this way, for these few times, we could nourish the very human need for deep connection that had been fractured by a global pandemic. In this way, we could benefit from and offer each other the gift of deep listening.

# One Small Step

Here's a question for you: If you had the chance to sit down and converse with a stranger who comes from a very different background, socio-economic status, race, political affiliation from you, would you do it? Would you know what questions to ask? Would you be able to listen for the story of what shapes their experience? Would you be open to having your own views of difference, your opinions, your biases impacted by what you hear?

As coaches, many of us would respond with a strong affirmative, and yet . . . as my decision not to sit down and talk with the MAGA guy on the park bench shows, there's much in the way of actually having that conversation.

Getting past the "stuff in the way" of these interactions is why One Small Step[15] was created. Similar to Craig's realization that birthed Make Shift Coffee House, the organizers of Story Corps[16] launched One Small Step to heal the divisions ripping us apart from one another – one conversation at a time.

Currently, One Small Step conversations are happening in the United States within four "anchor" communities: Wichita, Kansas; Oklahoma City, Oklahoma; Fresno, California; and Richmond, Virginia. Individuals outside those communities can apply to be matched with someone for these encounters on video. In addition, Story Corps partners with six public radio stations in Colorado, Tennessee, Georgia, North Carolina, Michigan, and Minnesota who conduct their own One Small Step programs.

These conversations are hosted by a trained facilitator, who will provide ground rules, orientation, and starting questions, such as ""Who has been the most influential person in your life? What did they teach you?" "Is there someone you disagree with but still love or respect?" "What are your fears or concerns about the future of our country?" With participant permission, the recorded interactions are then archived in the Library of Congress as a part of the American Folklife Center.[17]

With the enormity of misunderstandings currently afflicting our world, why would a few simple conversations make a difference? While I can certainly understand the fatigue behind that question, I'd like to share a painful experience of my own that I know would have benefited from facilitated conversation rather than the way it played out in a more public venue.

Earlier this year I was invited to an online performance by a Playback company in another part of the country. I was excited to see how this company would utilize a virtual platform for the audience. You may remember from earlier in this book that Playback is an art form where the performers "play back" true stories from the audience, with improvisation, movement, and music. The conductor for this experience had asked us – the viewers – for instances of difference in the sociometric opening. A few people had volunteered brief stories, and then there was a lull after the conductor asked for more. So I decided to unmute and speak up – at the same time that another viewer, a black man, spoke up. This gentleman graciously gave me the floor. I thanked him and offered my instance of difference. I didn't think anything of it until after the conductor asked for people to share feelings about how the previous segment had gone. The first woman to volunteer was a woman of color who said she felt frustrated that she did not get to hear from the black man who had given me the floor. She went on to say that this dynamic – a person of color stepping aside for a white person – was endemic in our culture, and she felt frustrated in seeing this play out yet again and being robbed of the story the man had to tell.

I felt myself stop breathing for a few seconds, as if I'd been slapped in the face. After I recovered a bit, a realization began to form. I had taken the man's graciousness at face value, when in fact, if I had understood the exchange from a wider perspective, I might have seen the implications more quickly. But the truth is, as a white person in America, my privileges include not having to widen my perspective, whereas people of color can't afford to ever narrow their own.

Learning is painful. Regardless of how anti-racist I may believe I am, if I am not aware, and can't own, that the scales have always been tipped in my direction, even as a woman, then I'm only adding to a pervasive and centuries-old scourge.

Now, if this situation, with stories from both sides, had played out in a privately facilitated One Small Step discussion, the learning here would most likely have been the same but perhaps without the shame inflicted on the participants. This shame, in these kinds of interactions, causes many CAUCASIANS to avoid these encounters at all. This avoidance fuels and calcifies division.

Clearly, we need to relearn how to listen with our hearts to build empathy. We need to remember how to use our ability to hear and process facts in a way that engenders trust. And we need to intentionally rebuild bridges of understanding over the chasms between us so that we can begin to heal our world.

I've applied via the One Small Step website to be matched for one of these conversations. Perhaps this story will inspire you to do the same.

# It's a Big Noisy World . . .

I wrote this book to encourage you to rethink your listening skills and tendencies, to get curious about how you and your clients listen to others, and to appreciate those with listening styles different from your own. It's my hope that I've given you some incentive to try on new ways of tuning in to the constant and multi-layered aural information that surrounds all of us. Consider this book an invitation to expand your perceptions and your intentionality in ways that benefit you in your very noisy professional and personal worlds.

On the following page, you'll find a list of resources: books, articles, websites that I found useful in advancing my own knowledge of this topic. I invite you to contact me anytime with questions, queries, or concerns at kym@kymdakin.com. To find out more about my work, please visit www.kymdakin.com.

Happy listening!

# Notes

1   *Wiser: Getting Beyond GroupThink to Make Groups Smarter*, Sunstein, C., Hastie, R., 2014
2   5 Qualities all Successful Leaders Have in Common: www.northeastern.edu/graduate/blog/top-5-leadership-qualities/2019
3   *Flowers of Rwanda: Making Peace with Genocide* (movie): https://bit.ly/3F7N9ad
4   Truth and Reconciliation Commission: www.justice.gov.za/trc/
5   Leadership and Organizational Studies, University of Southern Maine: https://usm.maine.edu/leadership
6   Restorative Justice Institute of Maine: www.rjimaine.org/
7   Accountability Factors in Restorative Justice: https://ojjdp.ojp.gov/sites/g/files/xyckuh176/files/pubs/implementing/accountability.html
8   *Jirga* (movie): www.imdb.com/title/tt7083846/

9   *The Upside of Uncertainty*, by Furr, Nathan and Harmon, Susannah, 2022
10  *Are Restorative Conferences Effective in Reducing Repeat Offending? Findings from a Campbell Systematic Review*, by Sherman, L.W., Strang, H., Mayo-Wilson, E., Woods, D.J., Ariel, B.: https://link.springer.com/article/10.1007/s10940-014-9222-9
11  Deep Canvassing, the Deep Canvass Institute: https://deepcanvass.org
12  The Listening Hour: www.listeninghour.org/
13  Jonathan Fox: www.linkedin.com/in/jonathan-fox-937298a/
14  Playback Theatre: www.playbackcentre.org
15  One Small Step: https://storycorps.org/discover/onesmallstep/
16  StoryCorps: https://storycorps.org/
17  Library of Congress: American Folklife Center: www.loc.gov/folklife/storycorpsfaq.html

# References

Azula Altucher, Claudia. *Become an Idea Machine*. Choose Yourself Media, LLC: 2015

Brown, Brené. *Rising Strong: The Reckoning. The Rumble. The Revolution.* AbeBooks: 2019

Busch, Christian. *The Serendipity Mindset*. Riverhead Books/Penguin Random House, LLC: 2020

Cameron, Julia. *The Artist's Way*. Jeremy Tarcher, Penguin Group: 1992

Chamine, Shirzad. *Positive Intelligence*. Greenleaf Book Group: 2012

Fox, Amaryllis. *Life Undercover: Coming of Age in the CIA*. Doubleday: 2020

Furr, Nathan and Susannah Harmon. *The Upside of Uncertainty*. Harvard Business School Publishing Corporation: 2022

Goulston, Mark. *Just Listen*. AMACOM: 2015

Jamison, Leslie. *The Empathy Exams*. Graywolf Press: 2014

Kuhnke, Elizabeth. *Persuasion and Influence for Dummies*. Wiley & Sons: 2012

Lee, Ingrid Fetell. *Joyful: The Power of Ordinary Things to Create Extraordinary Happiness*. Little, Brown Spark: 2018

Leonard, Kelly. *Yes, and: How Improvisation Reverses "No, but" Thinking and Improves Creativity and Collaboration*. Harper Collins Publishers: 2015

Murphy, Kate. *You're Not Listening and Why It Matters*. Celadon Books: 2021

Nordgren, Loran, and Schonthal, David. *The Human Element: Overcoming the Resistance That Awaits New Ideas*. Wiley: 2021

Ripley, Amanda. *High Conflict*. Simon & Schuster: 2022

Rohd, Michael. *Theatre for Community, Conflict & Dialogue*. Heinemann Educational Books, U.S: 1998

Rollnick, Stephen, PhD., and Miller, William. *Motivational Interviewing; Helping People to Change* (3rd edition). Guildford Press: 2012

Seo, Bo. *Good Arguments*. Penguin Random House: 2022

Stein Greenberg, Sarah. *Creative Acts for Curious People*. Random House: 2021

Sunstein, Cass and Hastie, Reid. *Wiser: Getting Beyond GroupThink to Make Groups Smarter*. Harvard Business Review Press: 2014

Treasure, Julian. *How to be Heard*. Mango Publishing: 2017
Walker, Rob. *The Art of Noticing*. Penguin Random House: 2019
Williams, Florence. *Nature Fix*. Norton, W. W. & Company, Inc.: 2018

# Additional References

Brown, Brené. *Daring Greatly: How the Courage to Be Vulnerable Transforms the Way We Live, Love, Parent, and Lead*. Penguin Publishing: 2015
Covey, Dr. Stephen R. *The Seven Habits of Highly Effective People*. Free Press: 1989
Gladwell, Malcolm. *Blink: The Power of Thinking Without Thinking*. Back Bay Books, Little, Brown: 2005
Goleman, Daniel. *Emotional Intelligence: Why It Can Matter More Than IQ*. Bantam Books: 1995
Lee, Harper. *To Kill a Mockingbird*. Harper Collins Publishers: 1960
Simmons, Annette. *The Story Factor: Inspiration, Influence, and Persuasion through the Art of Storytelling*. Basic Books: 2000
Zander, Rosamond Stone, and Zander, Benjamin. *The Art of Possibility*. Penguin Publishing: 2000

# Articles

"A Case History in Scientific Method" by B.F. Skinner, *American Psychologist*, 1956
"Carol Dweck Revisits the 'Growth Mindset'" by Carol Dweck, *Education Week*, 2015
"Creative Abilities in the Arts" by J.P. Guilford, *Psychological Review*, 1957
"Expressive Writing and Coping with Job Loss" by James Pennebaker, *JSTOR*, 1994
"Hardwired: The Brain's Circuitry for Political Belief" by Jonas T. Kaplan, *Science News*: December 2016
"The Liking Gap in Groups and Teams" by Adam M. Mastroiannia, Gus Cooney, Erica J. Boothby, Andrew G. Reece, *ScienceDirect*, 2022
"On Passion and Curiosity for Future Success" by Thomas Friedman, *Explo Blog*, February, 2013
"Overcoming Imposter Syndrome" by Gill Corkindale, *Harvard Business Review*, 2008
"Perfectionism Is Increasing over Time: A Meta-Analysis of Birth Cohort Differences from 1989 to 2016" by Thomas Curran and Andrew P. Hill, *APA PsycNet*, 2019

"Recognize the Creativity behind the Crime, Then You Can Thwart It" by David Cropley, *Psych Newsletter*, November 2020

"Tackling the Confirmation Bias Beast" by Joe Annotti, *TVNewsCheck*, 2022

"Want to Win Someone Over? Talk Like They Do" by M. Sytch, Y.H. Kim, *Harvard Business Review*, December 2020

# Websites

Are Restorative Justice Conferences Effective in Reducing Repeat Offending? https://link.springer.com/article/10.1007/S10940-9222-9, 2015

Assessment: What's Your Curiosity Profile? https://hbr.org/2015/12/assessment-whats-your-curiosity-profile

Association of Standardized Patient Educators: www.aspeducators.org/

Assume Positive Intent: https://collaborativeway.com/general/a-ceos-advice-assume-positive-intent/, 2017

Braver Angels: https://braverangels.org

Carol Dweck, Growth vs. Fixed Mindsets: https://fs.blog/carol-dweck-mindset/

Complicated vs. Complex Problems: https://tdan.com/complicated-vs-complex-problems/26066

Curiosity Quotient: Thomas Friedman: https://blog.explo.org/thomas-friedman-passion-and-curiosity-for-future-success, 2013

The Deep Canvass Institute: https://deepcanvass.org

EMDR Therapy: https://emdria.org/about-emdr-therapy/

Empathy Mapping Template: https://adobe.ly/3b5sG8V

The Fist by Dan Siegel: www.youtube.com/watch?v=gm9CTJ740xw, 2012

Good Group Decisions: https://craigfreshley.com

The Halo Effect: www.verywellmind.com/what-is-the-halo-effect-2795906

Harvard Implicit Bias Test: https://resources.lmu.edu/dei/initiativesprograms/implicitbiasinitiative/whatisimplicitbias/testyourimplicitbias-implicitassociationtestiat/

Health Education & Training Institute: www.hetimaine.org 5 Leadership Qualities: www.northeastern.edu/graduate/blog/top-5-leadership-qualities/

Library of Congress: The American Folklife Center, www.loc.gov/folklife/storycorpsfaq.html

Listening Hour: www.listeninghour.org

Listening Style Assessment Story YouTube: www.youtube.com/watch?v=OZNKWphsBfA

Make Shift Coffee House: https://makeshiftcoffeehouse.com

The Motivational Interview: https://psychologytoday.com/us/therapy-types/motivational-interview

Motivational Interviewing Certification Programs: https://bit.ly/3N6Kcb4

Motivational Interviewing Resources: https://bit.ly/3tbGXqO

North American Securities Administrators Association (NASAA): www.nasaa.org/4303/madoff-a-21st-century-ponzi-scheme/

North American Securities Administrators Association (NASAA): www.nasaa.org/about/

One Small Step: https://storycorps.org/discover/onesmallstep/

Playback Theatre: www.playbackcentre.org

Positive Intelligence: https://support.positiveintelligence.com/article/113-hyper-vigilant

Social Capital: www.britannica.com/topic/social-capital

Standardized Patient Program: www.aspeducators.org

Story Corps: https://storycorps.org/

Symptoms and Diagnosis of PTSD: www.verywellmind.com/requirements-for-ptsd-diagnosis-2797637

Waldorf Model of Early Childhood Education: www.waldorfeducation.org/waldorf-education

Whole Body Listening: https://study.com/learn/lesson/whole-body-listening-components-examples.html

# Acknowledgments

I find myself, since I embarked on this author journey, taking in the acknowledgments pages of the books I read. They are always filled with a gratitude that seems to radiate out of the pages, and now I have a visceral knowing as to the many reasons why.

There are a great number of people involved in "birthing" this book. First, for spawning the idea of writing a book at all, along with the oh-so-needed accountability structure, I must credit the amazing people involved in Seth Godin's Writing In Community, especially Michal Berman, Mark Brement, Lynn Carnes, Wendy Coad, Michael Cohen, Katy Dalgleish, Leanne Gordon, Kira Higgs, Julie Hughes, Kathy Karn, Diane Osgood, Pierre Powell, Titia Praamsma, Julie Rains, Joyce M. Sullivan, Kathy Taylor, and Terri Tomoff. I could never have had the fortitude to continue without the encouragement and excellent feedback of my beta readers: Joyce Bailey, Dave Collins, Meg Christie, Erin Curren, Nanette Giacomo, Margi Huber, David Lee, Christine Mallar, Michael Miles, Bill Maxwell, Michael Norton, Peggy Page, Marcia Pitcher, David Swardlick, and Mariah Wheeler. Carol Hess did a fabulous job with editing the first version and the book proposal.

My very dear friend and compatriot – Rahti Gorfein – deserves special thanks for bringing my book to the attention of Routledge, and at Routledge, I'm so grateful to Heather Evans for her vision, creative suggestions, and patience, as well as to Upasruti Biswas for her persistence and timely assistance.

And, of course, my small but very mighty, honest, and patient family: husband Rob Neal, for his many re-reads and excellent suggestions. My daughter Skyler, for contributing the excellent infographics to this book. I'm forever proud of her, and I can hardly wait to see what she does next!

# Index

# About the Author

Kymberly Dakin, MEd Adult Ed, mindset coach, and public speaker with Voice Into Learning, LLC. She is a founding company member of Portland Playback Theatre, an Audie winner for book narration, and creator of Shift/POV, a tool for deeper listening across difference. During the writing of this book, she co-developed the online bookmarking tool Nugget: to eliminate the need to take notes in online meetings. Teaching credentials: Bowdoin College, University of New Hampshire, University of Southern Maine, and University of New England. She lives in Maine, with weather known to encourage writing!

Printed in the United States
by Baker & Taylor Publisher Services